DISCIPLE

FAST TRACK

Remember Who You Are

THE PROPHETS
STUDY MANUAL

Dɪsᴄɪᴘʟᴇ FAST TRACK
The Prophets Study Manual
Copyright © 2018 by Abingdon Press
Dɪsᴄɪᴘʟᴇ: ʀᴇᴍᴇᴍʙᴇʀ ᴡʜᴏ ʏᴏᴜ ᴀʀᴇ
Study Manual, copyright © 1996 by Abingdon Press
All rights reserved.

Writers: Richard Byrd Wilke and Julia Kitchens Wilke
Consultant to the Writers: William J. A. Power
General Editors: Susan Wilke Fuquay and Elaine Friedrich

19 20 21 22 23 24 25 26 27 — 10 9 8 7 6 5 4 3 2
Manufactured in the United States of America

DISCIPLE FAST TRACK

CONTENTS

As You Begin DISCIPLE FAST TRACK   4

Chapter	Theme Word	
1. God's People Weep	Return	6
2. God Sent Messengers	Hear	14
3. Starved for the Words of the Lord	Hunger	22
4. God Pleads	Obey	32
5. God Rules the World	Divine Purpose	42
6. God Will Not Abandon	New Covenant	52
7. The Day of the Lord Has Come	Doom	60
8. God Cleanses and Renews	Promise	68
9. God Will Save	Redeemer	76
10. God's Vision for a New World	Vision	86
11. God's City of Peace	Courage	94
12. God's Mission for Israel	Witness	100

Timeline of Old Testament Biblical Events   109

Rulers and Prophets of Israel and Judah   110

Prophets of the Exile / Prophets After the Exile   110

Rulers of Neighboring Powers   111

As You Continue DISCIPLE FAST TRACK

You are beginning the third part of a four-part study. As you may know, DISCIPLE FAST TRACK: BECOMING DISCIPLES THROUGH BIBLE STUDY covered the whole Bible, Genesis through Revelation. DISCIPLE FAST TRACK: INTO THE WORD, INTO THE WORLD went deeper into Genesis and Exodus, Luke and Acts. This third study, DISCIPLE FAST TRACK: REMEMBER WHO YOU ARE, covers the Prophets and the Letters of Paul. The fourth study, DISCIPLE FAST TRACK: THE TREE OF LIFE, covers the Writings, John, and Revelation. So after completion of all four parts of the study, the Bible has been covered twice.

In this third study, you are entering familiar territory. The format of the Study Manual is familiar to you, though some features are new. They are explained below. Familiarity means you will be at home in the commitment you are now making of about thirty minutes a day for disciplined study and seventy-five minutes of participation in the group meeting.

The study is based on the Common English Bible (CEB). We recommend everyone have a study Bible because of the additional study aids included, such as explanatory notes and maps.

Daily Study

The amount of Scripture to be read daily varies from day to day and session to session. Some lessons require reading many chapters of Scripture; some sessions, fewer chapters. The important thing is to read and study daily. And taking notes as you read Scripture and listen to Scripture is an absolutely essential part of your daily study. Make it a daily habit also to read footnotes in your study Bible. When you begin studying a different book in the Bible, read the introduction to that book.

The Prophets

We will study the prophets in their historical sequence rather than in their biblical sequence. The prophets spoke in the context of history with its kings, nations, power struggles, and often brilliant achievements. So we pay attention to the history in order to understand the message of the prophets.

Often, more than one prophet is related to the same king. So each time we study a different prophet, we read about the king or kings to whom the prophet is related. And we read from a different perspective because each prophet is different and the relationship between the king and that prophet is set in a different context.

Much of the literature in the prophets is poetry. As you read, stay alert to word pictures and to symbolic meanings in the words. Look for the message under the words. Watch for words or phrases that signal connection to other events, persons, or situations.

The big backdrop for the prophets is God at work in history. Keep your eye on that.

Study Manual Format

The familiar elements of the Study Manual format are here. Two sections have different titles from the previous DISCIPLE FAST TRACK formats: The commentary section is titled "The Word of the Lord" and the discipleship or ministry section, "Marks of Obedient Community." The statement of "Our Human Condition" and the "Marks of Obedient Community" are always in tension. See them and struggle with them together. In line with the overall emphasis on community in this study, the "Marks of Obedient Community" section most often addresses the community rather than just the individual.

A new feature in DISCIPLE FAST TRACK: REMEMBER WHO YOU ARE is that each session in the Study Manual includes a "Context" section. This will help you understand the reading for each lesson. It tells you where the reading is taking place geographically, when it happens chronologically, and the kings and prophets involved. In addition, it gives you the living situation of the people. Be sure to read this section each week as you begin your daily reading.

Many suggestions in the "If You Want to Know More" section call for using additional Bible resources to study suggested topics and the maps in your study Bible or online.

Geography and history play a particularly important role in the lessons on the prophets. In nearly every group meeting, some work will involve using maps or a chart of history. There are resources in the back of this Study Manual that will help you with your understanding of the persons, places, and events important to the history or geography related to the lesson.

Individual research is not meant to result in a report to the group, though occasionally that may be appropriate. Rather, the exercise benefits the person who does it by equipping that person to bring the information into the discussion at appropriate points.

DISCIPLE

FAST TRACK

THE PROPHETS

"We must search and examine our ways;
we must return to the LORD."

—Lamentations 3:40

1 God's People Weep

OUR HUMAN CONDITION

We go our own way until we hurt. Then in shock and confusion we ask, What happened? With guilt we wonder, Where did we go wrong? We want to blame others. But confronted by the outcomes of our actions, we ask, Where can we turn for relief?

ASSIGNMENT

We begin by walking through the rubble of Jerusalem, reading Lamentations. Later, looking back through our tears, we will, week by week, read the warnings of the prophets. The grief, confusion, and hope we hear expressed in Lamentations we will hear also in the prophets. Now, read quickly the chapters from Deuteronomy to remember the life-and-death admonitions of Torah. Deuteronomy helps us know what went wrong. The destruction of Jerusalem and the exile into Babylon will forever shape our faith, as it has the faith of the Jews, for we will remember; we will repent; we will slowly envision a new future.

CONTEXT

Who
Jeremiah

Where
Jerusalem, Southern Kingdom of Judah

When
587/586 BC

Condition of the People
Jerusalem is desolate after being destroyed by Babylon. The Temple has been destroyed. Many of the Israelites are dead and most of their leaders have been marched into exile one thousand miles into the heart of the Babylonian Empire. They feel like the Lord has destroyed them and forgotten them.

Main Message
The prophet Jeremiah weeps over the destruction of Jerusalem. The kings and people of Israel had refused to believe that Jerusalem would ever be conquered. Yet King Nebuchadnezzar of Babylon succeeded. The nation of Israel is gone.

PRAYER

Pray daily before study:

"Hear my prayer, LORD!
    Listen closely to my cry for help!
Please don't ignore my tears!
I'm just a foreigner—
    an immigrant staying with you,
    just like all my ancestors were" (Psalm 39:12).

Prayer concerns for the week:

Day 1 Lamentations 1–3 (laments over Zion, God's warnings fulfilled, confession, God's steadfast love)

Day 4 Deuteronomy 12–18 (place of worship, warning against idolatry, sabbatical year, Passover, kingship)

Day 2 Lamentations 4–5 (punishment of Zion)

Day 5 Deuteronomy 23; 25–28 (miscellaneous laws, first fruits, altar on Mount Ebal, blessings and curses)

Day 3 Deuteronomy 5–11 (the Law at Sinai, a chosen people, warnings and consequences, God's requirements)

Day 6 "The Word of the Lord" and "Marks of Obedient Community"

Day 7 Rest, pray, and attend class.

THE WORD OF THE LORD

We are about to plunge into the prophets and the agony of Israel. The experience will be painful, filled with anguish and struggle. The prophets, in the name of God, will proclaim dire warnings, dramatize disasters to come—always pleading with the people to repent. When the people suffer, the prophets will weep. So will we.

We may become weary, reading the endless warnings. We may question our tightly held theologies. But the Word will never let the light go out.

The Agony in the Laments

Why begin this study with the Book of Lamentations? First, because our human tendency, like that of ancient Judah, is not to take shouts of warning seriously. But after reading Lamentations, we know the warnings were altogether fulfilled. The predicted punishment took place. So, when we read the prophets, we cannot be complacent.

Second, people often define their lives by some major event, a disaster or a life-shaping tragedy. The Jews can never forget that day in 587 BC when Babylon ravaged Jerusalem. Biblical theology is shaped by the day David's dynasty came to an end and Solomon's sanctuary was destroyed. Israel experienced a watershed of history when its people were slaughtered and survivors dispersed into foreign lands. Both Jews and Christians must read the Hebrew Bible through the eyes of postexilic Judaism.

Third, when you and I suffer grief, where can we go for help? We go to those who understand pain and sorrow because they have experienced it. We may cry, Is there any sorrow like my sorrow? What a relief to find others who hurt and who shake the doors of heaven for answers. In the depths of Israel's pain, we will find that the Lord who punishes is also the Lord who cares and sustains.

Anguish in History

The Assyrians had demolished the Northern Kingdom, first with a heavy invasion in 732 BC, then in 722 BC with siege, destruction, and exile. The Babylonians ravaged the Southern Kingdom with the same one-two punch—first an invasion in 597 BC and later in 587 BC following the awful siege, the complete destruction of Jerusalem. Jerusalem had believed itself to be impregnable. Now it lay in ruins.

Walk through the smoldering remains of the city in 587 BC. Step carefully over the broken stones and burning embers. Listen to the soft wails of raped women, starving children, mourning elders. Smell the stench. Young men and women able to walk were marched off into exile. A few scholars, some artisans, a handful of priests and nobility went into slavery with them. Just as Assyria had scattered Israelites from the Northern Kingdom over a century earlier, Babylon carted off the people of Judah from the Southern Kingdom after the siege of Jerusalem. The people of God had been slaughtered or scattered.

Solomon's Temple, carefully handcrafted centuries before, now lay in rubble, cedar beams smoldering amid the stones. In better days, the priests had offered there a continual stream of prayer and praise. Now the priests were dead or exiled, the gold and silver vessels carried away. Once during religious festivals, massive throngs gathered at the Temple. But now,

"Zion's roads are in mourning;
no one comes to the festivals" (Lamentations 1:4).

Walk into the Judean hills, a land of grazing and mixed farming. Crops had been confiscated or burned. The pastures were empty, for the animals had long since been eaten. Ancient landmarks were strewn about, homes and barns torn down. The Babylonians axed the centuries-old olive trees, set their stumps afire. They salted the fields so nothing would grow. Gone was the land of milk and honey, Abraham's promise, Moses' dream, Joshua's possession. The land was each family's inheritance. Gone was the land of promise.

The defeat marked the end of the monarchy. The king had become the sacred link between God and nation. The monarchy symbolized the body politic, uniting all the tribes of Israel into a cohesive nation. The golden age of David was recorded indelibly in the collective mind. When the Northern Kingdom, Israel, broke away after the death of Solomon, it was a tragic weakening of the nation. But the Southern Kingdom, Judah, carried on David's tradition. For four hundred years, each succeeding king had been a direct descendant of David, a sign of the providence and plan of God. Years before, Assyria had captured the last king of Samaria, putting an Assyrian governor in charge. Now David's descendant, King Zedekiah of Judah, was a prisoner. Babylon killed his sons while he watched, gouged out his eyes, and led the pitiable figure away into exile. With the collapse of the monarchy, God seemed to have abdicated divine protectorship, condemning Israel to the chaos of history.

Something happened to the soul of Judah. The theology of being a chosen people was tossed into turmoil. What had happened to God's protection? Judaism would spend generations trying to understand. Priests and prophets, wise leaders and ordinary people would thread theologies to make sense of catastrophe. Jewish and Christian communities continue the struggle to understand punishment and pain. It wasn't just that they were the chosen people, but that Josiah had instituted the reforms that Deuteronomy required. Deuteronomy had promised blessing for those who kept the commandments. But when Josiah was killed, the people had a crisis of faith, and when they were carried into exile, that crisis worsened.

Grief Laid Bare

Lamentations uses words that touch every human sorrow. The experiences are all voiced. *Shock:* The elders "sit on the ground and mourn" throwing "dust on their heads" (Lamentations 2:10). *Weeping:* Let "your tears stream down like a flood / all day and night" (2:18). *Bodily pain:* "My stomach is churning. / My insides are poured out on the ground" (2:11). *Loneliness:* "How lonely sits the city. . . . / How like a widow she has become. . . . / She weeps bitterly in the night" (1:1-2, NRSV). Notice the personification: The survivors are depicted as a bereaved woman. Judah or Jerusalem is a daughter, now in tears.

If any reaction is lacking, it is the normal effort to deny what actually happened. The destruction was so complete, the suffering so severe, that disbelief was impossible.

> "My soul continually thinks of it
> and is bowed down within me" (3:20, NRSV).

Like grieving people, Lamentations tells the details over and over. Guilt is expressed. So is shame. Self-pity is prevalent, and anger, projected toward God and others, explodes.

> "LORD, look and see to whom
> you have done this!" (2:20).

The writer demands that others must suffer (3:64).

Repentance is required, for we cannot be healed without it. "We are doomed / because we have sinned" (5:16). And with the healing balm of God's love comes the ability to trust again.

> "The LORD is my portion!
> Therefore I'll wait for him" (3:24).

Acceptance of reality and the willingness to go on help heal wounded souls.

> "Why then
> does any living person complain
> about their sins? (3:39).
> It's good to wait in silence
> for the LORD's deliverance" (3:26).

The Laments

A lament is a Hebrew poem, designed to verbalize suffering and pain, to be used at funerals, and to express grief within worship. Psalms 79 and 80 are laments. The prophetic books use laments as warnings—wailing, as it were, before the fact. The prophets sing the dirges long before the funeral.

Lamentations consists of five closely structured laments, one per chapter. They were meant to be chanted in worship. All around the world, Jews still read Lamentations on the ninth of Av (July/

NOTES

August) to remember the destruction of Solomon's Temple (587/586 BC) and the loss of the rebuilt Temple in AD 70. But the laments, like the Psalms, are meant to be read by anyone who needs to express sorrow. The poems employ every possible literary device to drive home pain and sorrow.

Prophetic Themes

The Israelites, in desperate straits, looked at their pitiable condition and asked, Why did this happen to us, God's chosen? Did God forget the promise to protect us from our enemies? Why did God destroy those things most sacred—the Temple, David's kingdom, Jerusalem, even take away the land of promise?

The questions escalate: Why have we been punished? For the sins of our mothers and fathers? for our own sins? Why was the punishment so harsh? Are we not the children of Abraham, the covenant people of Moses? Is there any hope at all for us?

For now, we can only hint at answers, for we have not yet probed the questions deeply. But Lamentations, like the prophets, agrees on several basic principles.

• *God is in charge.* There is no suggestion that God was weak, overwhelmed by other, more powerful gods or by some force of evil. No, clearly the events that happened were under God's control. Did God *allow* the destruction? Yes, for the lament says, God has withdrawn "his strong hand" (Lamentations 2:3), that is, pulled back his protective power. But more prominent is the insistence that God actually selected foreign armies to deliver divine punishment (1:14). The underlying conviction is that God punished Israel (1:15). God did not act casually or accidentally; God acted purposefully and intentionally.

• *The destruction was punishment.* "The crown has fallen off our head," a reference to both the fall of the king and the fall of the chosen nation; "We are doomed" (5:16).

The laments do not detail the sins and transgressions as the prophets do; they refer simply to rebellion. We will see this theme strongly dramatized by the prophets. But who sinned, forebears or the punished? Both, comes the answer. The ancestors were guilty. But the people suffered for their own sins as well. The experience was communal.

Did God forget Israel was special? No, God remembered. It was God's remembrance of righteousness that caused the destruction. The people forgot. They forgot Mount Sinai and Torah. The people of promise were special *within* the covenant. If they forgot the covenant, broke the commandments, forgot the poor, God would punish. Since nothing is more precious to God than justice and mercy, God would come down hard on injustice and cruelty, even if it meant destroying the Temple, the king, and the land of promise.

• *God has not abandoned Israel.* The despairing survivors, sitting in the ashes, cry plaintively, "Is this nothing to all you who pass by?" (1:12). Is there any hope for comfort? No, not from human sources. But the poets and prophets know God is never without new possibilities. The laments are laced with hope built on the dependability of God's Word.

> "The LORD has done what he purposed,
>   he has carried out his threat" (2:17, NRSV).

There is good news in that, for even God's punishment proves the Almighty is dependable.

God's Steadfast Love Will Yet Save

What can we do when hope seems gone, when even the voice of God is silent? In the heart of the laments we are told,

> "This I call to mind,
>   and therefore I have hope:
> The steadfast love of the LORD never ceases,
>   his mercies never come to an end;
> they are new every morning;
>   great is your faithfulness" (Lamentations 3:21-23, NRSV).

So Israel learns to trust the love that never ends, for "the LORD is good to those who wait for him" (3:25, NRSV).

In the fifth lament, the cadence of the poem turns to a major key: "Restore us, LORD, to yourself. / Please let us return! / Give us new days" (5:21).

Deuteronomy

Scholars say Deuteronomy is built on Mount Sinai, the Ten Commandments, the sermons of Moses, and the spiritual insights of Exodus and wilderness faith. But it was a living word, oral, and taught for centuries. Like all civil law, it received interpretation for new situations.

The point of Deuteronomy is that Moses made clear who the covenant people were and the God to whom they belonged. Moses told where the blessings would come from (28:1-14) and warned where the pitfalls lay (28:15-68).

At least part of Deuteronomy was in written form and found in the Temple during the reform of Josiah (620 BC). Reading it caused the king to repent and tear his clothes, for it showed how far Judah had strayed.

The book probably was finalized in Jerusalem after the Exile by the scholarly priests and prophets who returned from Babylon. The theology is clearly that of the prophets. It is as if Deuteronomy warned in advance from the time of Moses and then shouted "I told you so" after the destruction and exile. The rules for behavior were not new; they were drawn from the basic commandments. The Lord of the Hebrews pours forth justice (righteousness) and compassion. Stealing, adultery, false witness offend God's nature, violate the covenant community, and betray the harmony God desires for the world. A great responsibility rests on the shoulders of Israel.

NOTES

The prophets remember. They remember their beginnings. They remember the salvation event, and they know the conditions for survival. They understand Israel has a uniqueness, a special identity carefully prescribed by the Lord. So when the prophets speak, they compare what Israel is doing with what Israel is supposed to be doing. They give warning after warning, but Israel does not listen. All the counsel of Moses in Deuteronomy does not prevent the punishment.

Yet, God does not abandon the covenant people. Hints in Deuteronomy and glimmers of hope in Lamentations become full-blown visions in the prophets. God will bring the remnant home.

MARKS OF OBEDIENT COMMUNITY

The community of faith learns God's word is trustworthy. God means exactly what God says. When we remember God's law and God's love, we remember who we are and who we are meant to be. God judges, and God saves. So we can repent, realign our lives to God. We are never so lost as to be outside God's compassion. We can turn in confidence to God.

How do you understand the idea that the God who judges us, causing us pain, is also the God to whom we go for relief from that pain? What is your experience of this God?

Mark of Obedient Community
The community of faith relies on the trustworthiness of God's word.

How does your obedient community deal with suffering, especially suffering caused by sin or poor decisions?

When have you experienced "return"?

IF YOU WANT TO KNOW MORE

Pretend you just asked a grieving friend, "What happened?" and then reread Lamentations 4. Notice the attention to detail as the tragedy is recounted.

Read Deuteronomy 29–34 to hear Moses' third sermon, to understand the covenant better, to learn how Moses chose Joshua, and to hear Moses' final instruction and blessing.

> "Hear, O Israel: The LORD is our God, the LORD alone. You shall love the LORD your God with all your heart, and with all your soul, and with all your might. Keep these words that I am commanding you today in your heart."
> —Deuteronomy 6:4-6, NRSV

2 God Sent Messengers

OUR HUMAN CONDITION

We are drawn to the promises and practices of the culture that surrounds us. We try to walk in two worlds. We choose compromise—surely small compromises won't matter. A single loyalty asks too much. We look away; we don't want to hear.

ASSIGNMENT

We must know the history in order to understand the work of the prophets. We must hear them in context. We have much to read; so read quickly, noting important events and key figures. Associate prophets with their king counterparts and with the issue of conflict. Try to figure out what makes a prophet a prophet.

CONTEXT

Who and Where They Spoke
Nathan, Ahijah (United Kingdom)
Elijah, Elisha (Northern Kingdom)

When and Main Message
This session is an introduction to the prophets and covers the early prophets during the United Kingdom and the beginning of the Divided Kingdom.

Nathan: (1000-961 BC) Nathan reveals to King David his sins and urges repentance. He anoints Solomon.

Ahijah: (about 925 BC) Demonstrates the split of the United Kingdom of Israel before the kingdom divides by tearing his robe.

Elijah: (870-850 BC) Urges King Ahab and the people to return to the commandments of God.

Elisha: (850-800 BC) Continues Elijah's work in teaching a return to righteousness and faith.

PRAYER

Pray daily before study:

> "You've taught me since my youth, God,
>   and I'm still proclaiming your wondrous
>   deeds!
> So, even in my old age with gray hair,
>   don't abandon me, God!
>   Not until I tell generations about your
>   mighty arm,
>   tell all who are yet to come about
>   your strength" (Psalm 71:17-18).

Prayer concerns for the week:

Day 1 **Deuteronomy 6** (the Shema)**; 1 Samuel 8:1–10:16** (Samuel anoints Saul)**; 2 Samuel 12** (Nathan and David)

✓

Day 2 **1 Kings 11–14** (Solomon, Ahijah and Jeroboam, Shemaiah and Rehoboam)

✓

Day 3 **1 Kings 16:29–19:21; 21–22** (Elijah and Ahab, Micaiah and Jehoshaphat)**; 2 Kings 2**

✓

Day 4 **2 Kings 15–19** (Uzziah king of Judah, Ahaz, kings of Israel, Israel taken captive to Assyria, Hezekiah's reforms, Sennacherib invades Judah)

✓

Day 5 **2 Kings 20–25** (death of Hezekiah, Manasseh, kings of Judah, Josiah's reforms, fall of Jerusalem, Judah taken captive to Babylon)

✓

Day 6 **"The Word of the Lord" and "Marks of Obedient Community"**

Day 7 **Rest, pray, and attend class.**

DISCIPLE FAST TRACK

THE WORD OF THE LORD

No other civilization, no other religion ever produced people quite like the Hebrew prophets. Of course, sages and soothsayers, seers and fortune-tellers were scattered throughout the ancient world. Every tribe, every city, every nation had its gods and goddesses served by priests and prophets who conducted rituals, spoke in ecstatic language, even advised their rulers.

But the Hebrew prophets of the ninth, eighth, seventh, and sixth centuries BC were a different breed. Planted in the same Mediterranean soil as other nations, Israel produced prophets so disciplined, so determined to serve the God of Mount Sinai that they stand out with historic uniqueness.

Who Is a Prophet?

The Hebrew word *nabi*, translated "prophet," means simply "one who speaks for" or "one who represents." In the Bible, *nabi* means "one who speaks for God" or "God's messenger."

The word first appears in Scripture when King Abimelech called Abraham a prophet. The king perceived that Abraham and Sarah were in touch with God and on a special spiritual journey (Genesis 21:22). Moses was called a prophet unequaled among prophets (Deuteronomy 34:10-12). Both Abraham and Moses interceded for the guilty. Prophets speak to people for God and to God for people. Intercession is one of their primary functions.

Miriam was named a prophet when she sang God's victory song at the Red Sea (Exodus 15:20-21). Aaron was designated a prophet for Moses (7:1). On one occasion seventy elders "prophesied" standing at the tent of meeting (Numbers 11:25). Eldad and Medad, also elders, didn't go to the tent but "prophesied" anyway in the camp (11:26). Moses said he wished all the people were prophets like them (11:29).

Judges like Deborah, called a "prophetess," were in touch with God; but she was primarily an inspired executive and military leader (Judges 4:4-5, NRSV). The prophet Balaam, strange clairvoyant, gave divinely inspired forecasts of the outcome of battles to be. His temptation to sell out and the reprimand by his donkey illustrate the importance of prophetic integrity (Numbers 22–24).

Prophets and Kings

In many ways, Samuel was the first of the true prophets of Israel. His calling to be a prophet was clear and dramatic (1 Samuel 3:1-10). He performed one of the main duties of a prophet—to help Israel *remember its identity* and to *demand loyalty to the one God*. Like the great prophets to follow, Samuel dealt with the monarchy—warning, correcting, chastising, condemning. He anointed Saul (10:1), and later David (16:13), as king of Israel. Though he moved in and out of "schools" or groups of prophets, Samuel was God's prophet.

Some schools of prophets spoke in "prayer language." Saul joined them once, so that the saying went out "Is Saul also one of the prophets?" (10:10-13). But Samuel was never known for these ecstatic experiences. Though he did seem to have a special sense: He knew Saul's donkeys had been found (9:18-20). But the Bible indicates that the word *seer*, once used of Samuel, was no longer appropriate (9:9). Samuel's primary virtue was knowing and doing the will and work of God.

The Hebrew prophets were not fortune-tellers seeking information about future events by studying sheep's entrails. They didn't link people up with zodiac signs or determine their future from the stars. They weren't supposed to converse with the dead, although a medium did it once for King Saul (28:6-14). The law of Moses clearly forbade such practices (Deuteronomy 18:10-13).

We cannot define the prophets apart from the *monarchy*. We must know the actions of the kings if we are to understand the message of the prophets. Each king had schools of prophets attached to his shrine or living adjacent to his palace. They offered prayers, gave counsel—often "yes men" who said what the king wanted to hear. But in and out of that circle moved an occasional prophet who felt the call of God in his soul and spoke as if he were the holy God of Israel.

Nathan

The prophet Nathan was court adviser to King David. Whereas King Saul had listened to Samuel's continual stream of counsel, David said his own prayers, made his own decisions. Nathan was merely one of David's advisers—until King David saw Bathsheba bathing (2 Samuel 11:2-5).

When David's morality collapsed, Nathan the prophet came to the king. Using the subterfuge of telling a story about a poor man with a pet lamb, Nathan showed great courage (12:1-15). He lifted the role of prophet to a new and higher level as he looked King David in the eye and said, in effect, "You are an adulterer, murderer, thief, and liar." When Nathan said sternly, "You are that man!" (12:7), he was standing on the Ten Commandments given by God to Moses on Mount Sinai. What are some ways you experience godly confrontation for your actions?

The issue for Nathan was deeper than the king's breaking the commandments of God. The issue for Nathan was the king's breach of covenant. David had betrayed kingship by killing his soldier instead of protecting him, by stealing a man's wife instead of providing security for her home. He betrayed the trust of kingship by acting in self-interest. David sowed seeds of covenant deterioration that would one day bring down his monarchy.

Now look at Solomon, anointed by Nathan and the priest Zadok. What did King Solomon do wrong? He sealed treaties by marrying the daughters and sisters of foreign kings. Such intermarriage was expressly forbidden by Moses: "Don't intermarry with them" (Deuteronomy 7:3). Why? Because they would bring their pagan gods, their shrines, and their theologies with them, watering down God's Law. "They will definitely turn your heart toward their gods" (1 Kings 11:2). Worse, intermarriage would "turn your child away from following me so that they end up serving other gods" (Deuteronomy 7:4). What a denial of the great Deuteronomic command, "Recite them [the laws] to your children. Talk about them when you are sitting around your house and when you are out and about. . . . Write them on your house's doorframes and on your city's gates" (6:7-9).

From Solomon's idolatry flowed grievous sins—arrogance, greed, and misuse of his people. His opulent construction in Jerusalem raped land and people. In Solomon's old age, the nation trembled on the brink of revolution. Oppression had bred discontent. And at his death, the nation split between north and south.

Ahijah

The prophet Ahijah met Jeroboam on a lonely road near Jerusalem, and Ahijah tore his new robe into twelve pieces (1 Kings 11:29-39). Then, to Jeroboam, a non-Davidic, Northern "commoner" who had served as superintendent of forced labor for Solomon, the prophet gave ten pieces of his robe. His gift represented the ten tribes that would become the Northern Kingdom, to be called Israel. He withheld two pieces of his robe (presumably for Benjamin and Judah) for King David's sake and for Jerusalem's sake to symbolize the Southern Kingdom, to be called Judah (11:32).

Ahijah's symbolic action did three things—spotlighted sin, forecast the future, and helped to bring the future to pass. The civil breach took place without a single blow struck. Another prophet, Shemaiah, stopped Solomon's son Rehoboam from going to war against the new Northern Kingdom by saying, "This is what the LORD says: . . . this is my plan" (12:24). And 180,000 Judean soldiers went home without a fight.

Like the prophets to follow, Ahijah wanted Jerusalem to be the one and only center of worship, even though he recognized political division. Unfortunately, King Jeroboam of the Northern Kingdom determined that political unity demanded national shrines. He installed worship centers with calves of gold in Bethel and Dan and set the stage for ultimate disaster. From then on, when historians wanted to refer to idolatry, they used shorthand— "the sins of Jeroboam."

Elijah

Do not lose sight of these key points—the interaction between prophet and king, the concern of the prophet for a faithful monarchy, and the prophetic effort to maintain the laws and the land. Kings were meant to be shepherds of Israel, serving in God's behalf. The prophets, with courage and consistency, denounced the kings whenever they violated this charge.

Just as King David had his prophet Nathan, so King Ahab of the Northern Kingdom had Elijah. The baggage of divinations, ecstatic language, even miracles of healing, seemed incidental to Elijah. He knew he was God's messenger to help Israel remember that the Lord is God and to return to the covenant.

The contest against the 450 priests of Baal was not a game for Elijah. It was life and death for Israel (1 Kings 18:17-46). Either Israel belonged to God, or it did not. Either the covenant was in effect, or it was not. If the first commandment were broken, all other commandments would be broken as well. Salvation memory was at stake. Identity as God's chosen people was at stake. The Promised Land was at stake. Idolatry is the enemy on Mount Carmel. Idolatry is the Number One sin. It is so hard for us to recognize our own idolatry when our idols do not have faces of stone or gold. But it was also hard for ancient Israel to understand. They couldn't fathom that a seemingly innocent mixing of gods could be such a threat. The baals had great power, because they diluted loyalty to God and watered down law and grace.

What gods from our surrounding culture do we adopt and allow to dilute our loyalty to God?

Ahab had married Jezebel from the royal family in Sidon to seal a treaty with the seafaring Phoenicians. Jezebel brought with her all her pagan gods and an entourage of cultic prophets. The queen was trained in royal ways: The monarchy was absolute. You hired your prophets, you prayed to the gods for success, and you did as you pleased. Ahab, trained in the ways of Israel, knew in his heart that God had given each Hebrew a piece of land; that everyone, even the king, stood under the Ten Commandments; and that the king was supposed to be shepherd-servant for the people.

When Ahab wanted a little garden plot near the palace, Jezebel had its owner, Naboth, killed; and she gave the land to Ahab (21:1-16). Her gods did not care. They dealt with fertility issues like rain and childbirth, with victory in war, with protection from injury and disease. They made no moral demands.

King Ahab lived with compromise, worshiping both God and Baal, listening to Israel's prophets as well as to foreign prophets. "So you've found me, my old enemy!" (21:20) are words of both guilt and awe. Elijah's words about Naboth's vineyard pricked Ahab's heart. He knew prophets spoke for God.

A true prophet was one whose words rang true, whose predictions came to pass. Elijah said, "Dogs will devour Jezebel" (21:23). His words were fulfilled when Jehu's horses crushed her body and the dogs devoured her (2 Kings 9:30-37). The prophet Micaiah, alone and in opposition to four hundred court prophets, decreed disaster in battle for King Ahab (1 Kings 22:13-28). The court prophets ridiculed Micaiah and one slapped him, but the kings expected Micaiah to speak God's truth. When an arrow pierced a space in Ahab's armor, the prophet's words came true (22:34-35).

Elisha

Elijah's mantle, with a double share of his spirit, was passed to Elisha (2 Kings 2:9-14). Notice two attributes apparent in the prophet Elisha—his compassion for the poor and his ministry to foreigners. Elisha, often in the company of a group of prophets, learned that a widow of a prophet was destitute. Creditors were coming to take her two children into slavery. God, through Elisha, wondrously provided enough oil so she could pay her debts (4:1-7). Concern and care for the weak was basic to Torah (Deuteronomy 24:12-15, 17-21).

Elisha healed an Aramean commander, Naaman, who had leprosy. Naaman tried to pay him, but Elisha refused to accept money—a fact that characterized the great prophets of Israel. They could not be bought or bribed. They were determined to act without shadow of compromise (2 Kings 5). Read 2 Kings 5:13-14. What examples can you think of where God's healing may be simple, but we make it complicated?

Called to Be Messengers

So what shall we say about the prophets? They believed they were called of God to be messengers at any risk to themselves. They were people of unswerving devotion to God as they remembered ancestral promises and Mosaic principles. By word and symbolic action they challenged kings to total allegiance to God. Their words rang true, their warnings fulfilled. With unspeakable courage, they condemned idolatry, knowing it would cloud collective memory and soften the nation's sense of justice. Idolatry would lead to immorality. Fiercely the prophets pleaded for a return to God lest the monarchy fail, lest the God who had saved them be forced to punish them.

The prophets held in their memories God's actions in the past—freedom from slavery, providential care each day in the wilderness, clear laws for harmonious community, and a land of promise where each family would live on its inheritance with justice and compassion. Then they read the signs of their times and courageously portrayed the truth for others in every conceivable way. Unfortunately, most people either refused to see and hear or were unwilling to pay the price of obedience.

MARKS OF OBEDIENT COMMUNITY

Loyalty to the one God characterizes obedient community. And loyalty is kept intact through our collective memory. What does it mean to think about these same challenges of loyalty to God in your community of faith?

Mark of Obedient Community
The obedient community chooses loyalty to God as its first commitment.

The prophets knew that Israel must belong totally to God or it was lost. So, like the prophets, we must understand idolatry, that tendency we have to stray to other loyalties. We know that false gods will destroy us.

Obedience to God's teaching is at the heart of loyalty to God. Yet in modern society we often want to avoid both the word *obey* and the idea of *obedience*. Why?

How does collective memory encourage the community to be obedient?

IF YOU WANT TO KNOW MORE

Several terms are used for the prophets and the biblical books named for prophets:

- *Major Prophets*—in the Christian canon, Isaiah through Daniel
- *Minor Prophets*—Hosea through Malachi; the terms *Major* and *Minor* refer to length, not to importance of the books
- *Preexilic Prophets*—those who prophesied before the Exile or whose writings addressed Israel and Judah before the Exile
- *Postexilic Prophets*—those who prophesied after the Exile or whose writings addressed the people of Judah after the Exile

"The days are surely coming, says the LORD God,
when I will send hunger and thirst on the land;
neither a hunger for bread, nor a thirst for water,
but of hearing the LORD's words."

—Amos 8:11

3 Starved for the Words of the Lord

OUR HUMAN CONDITION

We often go our own way in times of prosperity. We worship other gods. We take advantage of the poor. We are divided in our loyalties. Then when consequences come, we seek help from God, but get silence. Where is God's assurance? What can fill this emptiness?

ASSIGNMENT

First, skim Amos, getting a feel for the overall message. Then read carefully, deliberately. Hosea was a long-time prophet active during the reigns of various kings. As you read 2 Kings 15, identify one or two acts of each king.

Like other prophets, Hosea can be scathing. Yet Hosea's pathos, his compassion, can be as tender as a mother's kiss, as gentle as a lover's touch.

CONTEXT

Who
Amos (from the Southern Kingdom of Judah)
Hosea (from the Northern Kingdom of Israel)

Where They Spoke
Northern Kingdom of Israel

When
About 150 years after the United Kingdom of Israel divides (about 783 BC to 742 BC).

Condition of the People
A time of peace and prosperity for the wealthy of both kingdoms in spite of their idolatry and immorality.

Main Message
Amos: God is going to punish the Northern Kingdom of Israel for worshiping in the Temple and then going out and oppressing the poor. Worship was to lead them to reflect God to the world. They were worshiping while they were perverting justice and righteousness. This was defiling worship through their actions of oppression and immorality.

Hosea: The Northern Kingdom, Israel, has committed idolatry and failure to love God.

PRAYER

Pray daily before study:

"So now you, LORD—
    don't hold back any of your compassion
        from me.
Let your loyal love and faithfulness always
    protect me" (Psalm 40:11).

Prayer concerns for the week:

Day 1 Amos 1–5 (judgment on Israel's neighbors, Judah and Israel)

✓

Day 2 Amos 6–9 (the day of the Lord, visions of judgment, Amaziah, no escape from judgment)**; 2 Kings 14:23-29** (Jeroboam II)

✓

Day 3 Hosea 1–6 (Hosea's marriage to Gomer, faithless Israel, God accuses Israel, coming judgment on Israel and Judah)

✓

Day 4 Hosea 7–11 (futile reliance on other nations, chastisement of Israel, Israel's sin and captivity)

✓

Day 5 Hosea 12–14 (Israel's sin, Lord's anger against Israel, repentance brings blessing)**; 2 Kings 15:1-31** (Uzziah king of Judah, various kings of Israel)

✓

Day 6 "The Word of the Lord" and "Marks of Obedient Community"

Day 7 Rest, pray, and attend class.

THE WORD OF THE LORD: AMOS

Tekoa was a small Judean village six miles south of Bethlehem. The town sat on a ridge that separated the rocky pastures and marginal cropland on the north from the barren Negeb wilderness on the south. The terrain was harsh, breeding independent, hard-working people like Amos.

Amos was a shepherd, but he also tended an inferior kind of fig tree called a sycamore fig that required a careful prick of the emerging fruit to allow it to ripen clean and insect free, making it edible. Not like the lush figs from the Jezreel Valley, this fig was eaten by the poor and fed to animals.

This shepherd-farmer did not belong to a school of prophets, was not linked to a sanctuary, was never paid for prophecy. Without credentials, he proclaimed, "I am not a prophet, nor am I a prophet's son" (Amos 7:14). Yet God said to him, "Go, prophesy to my people Israel" (7:15).

Go to Bethel

Amos carried the stigma of a southerner going north, a Judean intruding into Israel's affairs. He was obligated to announce destruction and death—not a happy task. But worse, he had to preach doom and gloom when most Israelites were basking in success and believing God was blessing them richly.

Now, if Amos were to travel into the Northern Kingdom to deliver one searing sermon, where would he go? To Bethel, of course, the king's shrine, the house of the priest, the center of idolatry. So Amos walked six miles to Bethlehem, another six to Jerusalem, then up the trader's trail, crossing the Judah-Israel border, eleven more miles to Bethel.

Bethel was steeped in tradition. Abraham pitched his tents there (Genesis 12:8; 13:3). Jacob dreamed of God, set up a sacred pillar of rock, and named it Bethel, "God's house" (28:10-22). Samuel made annual pilgrimage to its sanctuary (1 Samuel 7:16), and in the days of Elisha a school of prophets lived there (2 Kings 2:3).

When the kingdom divided (922 BC), Jeroboam son of Nebat thought it necessary to have the people of the north worship at national shrines, Bethel and Dan, rather than go to the Temple in Jerusalem (1 Kings 12:25-30). No sooner had Jeroboam designated Bethel a royal sanctuary than he added a golden calf, full of fertility cult meanings. The mixing of Egyptian, Canaanite, and Hebrew religious concepts watered down Torah, violated the laws of Sinai, and spawned idolatry so feared and hated by the prophets. Now, centuries later, as Amos would show, that idolatry led to injustice and immorality (Amos 5:4-7).

What kind of worship would lead us to bring about justice and righteousness?

Speaking for God

Amos lived during the reign of two great kings, Uzziah of Judah (783–742 BC) and Jeroboam II of Israel (786–746 BC). Under these long-tenured monarchs, except for occasional border disputes, the period was tranquil and both tiny nations flowered.

Foreign powers were struggling with internal problems or fighting with enemies on other fronts. Egypt, after earlier military expansion, had slipped back into its own Nile Valley. Syria, with its capital Damascus still flourishing, nevertheless watched neighboring nations nip at its outlying territories. The Assyrian Empire floundered under weak kings. So with the superpowers Egypt and Assyria asleep and Syria threatened, Israel saw a window of opportunity and pushed its boundaries toward the north, east, and south. Trade flourished because all the main trade routes from Mesopotamia to Egypt passed through Israel's toll stations. People thought themselves quite religious, honoring Hebrew festivals, presenting gifts to Canaanite gods, giving tithes, offering prayers, and celebrating their blessings.

If Jeroboam II had run for office in mid-eighth century BC, his slogan would have been "Peace and Prosperity." Israel basked in a golden moment. Pride and plenty ruled the land. Cities sparkled with elegance. The rich enjoyed both winter and summer homes, decorating their bedsteads with inlaid ivory, adorning their couches with damask pillows. They entertained one another with sumptuous feasts. Wine was not only sipped at meals but guzzled at orgies. The men slipped money under the table. The women grew greedy and demanding.

Into this arena strode the Southern shepherd. In front of the priest Amaziah, a school of prophets, and an assortment of business and civic leaders, Amos proclaimed God's coming judgment. He pointed first to Syria, Israel's hated neighbor, announcing that the Judge of all nations would destroy the brutal king Hazael and his son Ben-hadad (Amos 1:3-5).

Next came Gaza, the seacoast home of ancient enemies, the Philistines (1:6-8). Fire would fall upon cities named for their gods, Ashdod and Ashkelon. Amos spoke of Tyre, the upper coastal region, often friendly, sometimes politically allied, occasionally intermarried (1:9-10).

Now the sermon began to hit home. Amos denounced his own homeland, Judah, separate but still Hebrew (2:4-5). He recalled God's saving actions, going back to Moses and Egypt, to Joshua and victory over the Amorites. Judah's history was Israel's history too. Amos said Judah had rejected the law of the Lord (2:4). But, thought the people, Jerusalem has sacrifices in the Temple. Judah had been led astray by lies (2:4). But, thought the listeners, they study the law of Moses.

Now Amos did what he came to do. In God's name he took aim at Israel. Their prosperity was built on the backs of the poor. You "have sold the innocent for silver, / and those in need for a pair of sandals" (2:6). You "crush the head of the poor into the dust of the earth" (2:7). How? With inequities. You "take a bribe" so the poor do

DISCIPLE FAST TRACK

not receive justice. In fact, you shove them aside at the court (the gate of the city) (5:12, NRSV). The law of Moses said, "Cursed is anyone who obstructs the legal rights of immigrants, orphans, and widows" (Deuteronomy 27:19).

Sometimes religious people today give food baskets to the poor but create social structures that oppress them. What are some economic devices that steal from the poor?

Under covenant law, the disabled were to be given special consideration. Your sexual sins defy the laws of God. You teach serious-minded young people—youth you might have nurtured—to break their holy vows. You who are prophets and priests, fathers and mothers, you should be teaching the words of God; but you are neglecting your task. You silence your preachers who might bring you back to God (Amos 2:11-12).

A famine is coming, said Amos, "not a famine of bread, or a thirst for water, / but of hearing the words of the LORD" (8:11, NIV).

"On that day the . . . young women and the young men will faint with thirst. . . . / They will fall and never rise again" (8:13-14).

What do you think it would be like to hunger for God's words and not be able to hear them? *exile*

Greed controls your lives, claims Amos. You can hardly wait for Sabbath to end so you can begin making money again. You are eager for religious festivals to finish so you can get back to work (8:5). You have turned a blessing into a curse and a curse into a blessing. Your rich people lavish comforts on themselves while the homeless go hungry in the streets.

When you go to worship, your heart is not in it. You go to Bethel with guilt on your hands and greed in your hearts. You love to make offerings, give tithes, and sing songs, but you are not in love with the God of Sinai (4:4-5). When God drops the plumb line alongside you—your attitudes and actions—you will be shown up as crooked (7:7-8). Nothing is so unforgiving as a plumb line; it reveals every distortion.

Because worship had become hypocrisy, because the sacrifices at the altar were separated from the sanctity of justice and compassion, God cried out through Amos:

NOTES

"I hate, I reject your festivals,
    I don't enjoy your joyous assemblies. . . .
Take away the noise of your songs. . . .
But let justice roll down like waters,
    and righteousness like an ever-flowing
        stream" (5:21-24).

When does our worship become empty ritual rather than obedience to God?

The saddest part for God was that Israel was so special. God judges all the nations, but Israel was God's pride and joy. Nevertheless, Amos must prophesy against Israel.

The Day of the Lord

Just as a trumpet (ram's horn) calls a city to emergency, so the prophet announced God's forthcoming actions (Amos 3:6-8). Because the people had been given special privileges (the Law, the covenant, the salvation history), they would be given severe punishment for their unfaithfulness. They boasted about "the day of the Lord" when they thought God would bring restoration of David's kingdom, peace, and victory for Israel. Amos turned understanding of the expression "the day of the Lord" upside down.

Amos publishes the obituary in advance, relentlessly repeating the message. Israel is drawing inexorably to its end. How soon will it come? Like summer fruit, it is dead ripe (8:1-3). The Hebrew uses a fearful pun; *qayits* (fresh fruit) sounds like *qets* (end). The end of Israel is near.

But *will* Israel repent? No. They are apostate, unfaithful. So the God "who made the Pleiades and Orion," who recreates each day afresh, who draws from the ocean to give us rain and thus sustains life, will make "destruction to flash out against the strong" (5:8-9).

Notice three aspects of God's response to Israel's idolatry and injustice.

• *God's thoughts.* God looks over the situation and is offended. God smells the stench of injustice, robbery, disenfranchisement, poverty, and enslavement.

• *God's instruments.* God does not act directly. Instead, God uses agents to punish. The soil turns against the people (8:8); the earth shakes (9:1, 9); the locusts devour (4:9). Enemy nations destroy. Assyria will be God's punishing rod against a transgressing Israel (7:9, 11).

• *God cannot deny reality.* Human deceit destroys community. Sin breaks down the network of society.

Disciple FAST TRACK

THE WORD OF THE LORD: HOSEA

Hosea's book is filled with difficulties. Certain Hebrew words are obscure. Poetic allusions have distant meanings. Ancient editors have reworked the text. The book collects Hosea's oracles, sermons, laments, symbolic actions, poems, and explanations. All are loosely bound together without strict chronology or continuity.

Hosea was a contemporary of Amos. But he did not carry Amos's stigma of coming to the north from the south. Hosea spoke to his own beloved people, Israel. Nor did he confine his work to one trumpet blast at Bethel. Hosea prophesied for more than twenty years. Like Amos, he preached during the prosperity and peace of Jeroboam II but continued into the period of confusion, anarchy, and destruction afterward. Unlike Amos, who was sent packing after his pronouncements, Hosea not only announced desolation; he also watched as it transpired.

He continued to prophesy as Jeroboam's son Zechariah (not the prophet) was killed by Shallum after a six-month reign. Within one month, Shallum was killed by Menahem, who ruled for seven years fighting Assyria. His son Pekahiah was murdered by one of his officers, Pekah, who ruled five years. Hosea preached while Israel was falling apart.

Remember, the prophets have two overarching spiritual enemies—injustice and idolatry. Amos focused more on social injustice, the breakdown of human relationships. Hosea pointed more to idolatry, the failure to love God. The two issues, love of neighbor and love of God, are opposite sides of the same coin (Hosea 4:1-2).

Unfaithful

The descriptions of Hosea's wife, Gomer, are confusing.

Hosea 1 is written as biography; Hosea 3, as autobiography. Was Gomer a prostitute before Hosea married her, or simply a woman with a tendency to be unfaithful (1:2)? Did she become a woman of the streets or a prostitute at the shrine of the baals? Did God's love for Israel induce Hosea to buy his wife back, or did Hosea's unrequited love for her teach him about God's unbounded mercy? No matter. In this experience of marital infidelity, Hosea felt the broken heart of God over God's unfaithful people. In the cost of bringing Gomer home, Hosea understood that God would never abandon Israel, no matter the price.

Here, early in the prophets, the marriage between a man and a woman is compared to the love relationship between God and God's people. In fact, the allegory in Hosea 2 is so interwoven that often we cannot tell if we are dealing with Hosea and Gomer or with God and Israel.

Today the prophet's picturing his wife's unfaithfulness as a symbol of Israel's unfaithfulness might be interpreted as debasing womanhood. We would hesitate to use such an analogy. Still the image of a broken marriage drives home to us the prophetic message of the brokenness between God and Israel.

Look carefully at Hosea 2. Gomer ran to other lovers, probably as a cult prostitute at Bethel or Gilgal or Dan. Hosea's heart was broken. She was his beloved, the mother of his children. He asked two of the children, now called "My People" and "Compassion," to plead with their mother to come home (2:1-2), but to no avail. Would Israel ever repent? Not until the nation was punished, for her feeble efforts to change were always like the early morning dew, quick to vanish (6:4).

What Were the Baals?

The baals were nature gods. Baal was god of the storm, the wind, and the rain. In a land desperate for rain as the source of life, where the slightest failure meant drought and famine, the people were drawn to Baal worship.

Worship consisted of going to the "high places," a pillar or tree on a hilltop, and trying to placate these fertility gods and goddesses. Worship included offerings of agricultural produce— wool, flax, olive oil, wine, grain, bread, and water (Hosea 2:5, 9). Sometimes, in desperate appeals, firstborn children were offered. The prophets were aghast, but occasionally even an Israelite king would cause his firstborn to "pass through fire," a euphemism for child sacrifice.

Why Worship the Baals?

Why were people drawn to these fertility gods? Life was so precarious, so fragile in Canaan. Rainfall was marginal and uncertain. Grasshoppers, locusts, and windstorms could destroy a crop. Families could not feed themselves or maintain their little flocks of sheep and goats.

If you thought it might help your farm feed your babies, and if you could still offer sacrifices to the God of Abraham, wouldn't you go to the high places of Canaan? When people had sexual intercourse with the sacred prostitutes beside the bull of Baal and the pillar of Asherah, they reenacted the drama of the gods, which, they believed, released power to guarantee fertility. In a nonscientific age, a farmer dared not ignore Baal rites that could have an impact on his future. In a nearly powerless predicament, how could people gain some semblance of control?

What Was the Result?

Of course the prophets hated the worship of false gods, pillars, and images. Of course Hosea was offended by the sexual interchange that violated the strict laws of Moses on marriage and family. But still more tragic, Baal worship gave devotees a sense that "God is with us." The establishment used Baal worship as a way of maintaining the status quo. The nobility and priests reinforced their own power and influence without divine condemnation—in fact, with support from the gods. Not only would they lose sight of God's rule—the way the world really runs—but they would try to run the world another way, their way, the way of elbowing a neighbor and oppressing the weak.

DISCIPLE FAST TRACK

The net result was not the harmony and fertility the people hoped for. The people were running away from the God of order and running toward the ways of confusion. The prophets knew that idolatry led to immorality. Immorality shattered community. The people, by worshiping false gods, would destroy themselves by "swearing, lying, murder, / together with stealing and adultery" (4:2). Even the soil (which they had tried to make fertile) turned unproductive: "the earth itself becomes sick, / and all who live on it grow weak" (4:3).

The Kings

The priests encouraged the kings and other officials to flirt with foreign alliances. A pro-Assyrian party and a pro-Egyptian party believed Assyria or Egypt could help them (Hosea 5:13; 8:9; 12:1). When Assyria was weak, Israel fought against Aram (Syria), centered in Damascus. Later, in 734–733, Israel and Syria joined forces to build a coalition against Judah and were encouraged by Egypt.

Did you notice that Hosea did not name the kings of Israel he served after Jeroboam II died (1:1)? He named the kings of Judah for the next several years. Why? Four of the five kings of Israel were assassinated in those years. They usurped the throne by violence. No Samuel came to anoint a king like David. No Nathan came to anoint a king like Solomon. God was not even consulted.

Punishment

Cause and effect—that's how Hosea saw it. The more Israel, the vineyard of God, flourished, the greater became the idolatry (10:1). You made the calf to worship; you shall carry the calf (as exiles) to Assyria (10:5-6). You didn't let God choose your kings; the kings will float away like a chip on the water (10:7). You plow wickedness; you reap depravity (10:13). Gomer broke the bonds of marriage; she ended up in the chains of slavery. You sow the wind, and you reap the whirlwind (8:7).

Redemption

Would God forsake Israel? No, that would be impossible. Forsaking Israel would violate the steadfast love of God. Could Hosea abandon Gomer? No, he bought her back for fifteen pieces of silver, a large amount of barley, and a portion of wine (Hosea 3:2), a highly symbolic figure, equivalent in money and produce to the thirty shekels prescribed by the Law as the full and proper value of a woman given as a vow to God (Leviticus 27:4). For a symbol of a bedraggled Israel, Hosea paid top price to show how much he valued her. The cost of redemptive love is high.

MARKS OF OBEDIENT COMMUNITY

We know we are nourished by the words of the Lord. They are our bread and milk. Without the word, our community starves. We lose our memory, our identity, our guide, our hope.

Mark of Obedient Community
The faithful, obedient community lives on, lives in, and lives by the words of the Lord. They declare the redeeming love of God calling people back to God.

Surely there is "hunger and thirst on the land" today. How would you describe it?

Amos warned that the faithlessness of the people would result in God's withdrawing his word from them. A judgment of famine. God could be reached only through repentance.

What faithlessness in us and in our community of faith would today bring Amos's warning that God would have nothing more to say to us?

We know we belong to God. We know God loves us, provides for us, comforts us like a parent loves a child, like a lover loves a mate. We know there are "baals" that would draw us into infidelity; but today they are not idols of wood or stone, so they are hard to spot. Today's false gods are subtle, but we know we are tempted by them. Today we even find it hard to grasp the concept of idolatry because our false gods look so different and have different names.

What becomes idolatry for the community of faith today?

How might we be bringing our gods into our worship of God, deceiving ourselves about what we are doing?

What sources of strength help us resist idolatry and focus on righteousness?

IF YOU WANT TO KNOW MORE

In a Bible dictionary, look up Jeroboam I son of Nebat and Jeroboam II son of Joash. Compare their policies.

The prophets preached against the backdrop of history and geography, kings and nations. As you come across names of kings, countries, and cities, read about them in a Bible dictionary or Bible atlas. For example, Hazael, Ben-hadad, Aram, and Damascus.

"Therefore, as a tongue of fire devours stubble,
 and as hay shrivels in a flame,
  so their roots will rot,
  and their blossoms turn to dust,
 for they have rejected the teaching of the LORD of heavenly forces,
  and have despised the word of Israel's holy one." —Isaiah 5:24

4 God Pleads

OUR HUMAN CONDITION

When confronted with our injustice in our daily dealings, we defend it or explain it away by comparing it to other injustices. We offer promises to change our ways and believe we will be forgiven, not punished. We block out all mention of judgment. We don't want anyone pleading with us to change our ways.

ASSIGNMENT

As you read, be aware of the changing political landscape and the economic and social realities that caused the prophets to speak out.

One note of explanation: Usually the prophet's time frame is established by naming *Judah's* king (Davidic) even if *Israel* (Northern Kingdom) is discussed.

In Micah, listen for echoes of Mount Sinai and Torah.

Isaiah 1–39 seems to be pre-Exile prophecies covering several decades in the eighth century BC.

Notice that messianic prophecies come when times seem dark, hope almost gone.

CONTEXT

Who
Micah and Isaiah: Both prophets from the Southern Kingdom, Judah.

Where
Micah and Isaiah speak to both kingdoms, but especially to those in Jerusalem, the capital of Judah.

When
Between 750 and 686 BC.

Condition of the People
These prophets are born in a time of peace and prosperity, especially for the wealthy. There is growing apostasy in both nations. Then in 746 BC, the Northern king, Jeroboam II, dies. In 742 BC, the Southern king, Uzziah, dies. This begins a period of instability with several more evil kings in both Israel and Judah. At the same time, a great leader of nearby Assyria, Tiglath-Pileser III, known as Pul, is gaining power. Two prophets, Micah and Isaiah, enter the scene. They warn the people during this tumultuous time.

Main Message
Micah: Because of idolatry and injustice, God is going to allow other nations to destroy both Israel and Judah. People will be killed and exiled. Someday God will bring God's people back to rebuild Jerusalem.

Isaiah: God is patient but will eventually send consequences for sin, not for the purpose of punishment but to drive people to repentance.

PRAYER

Pray daily before study:

> "Please, LORD,
>   don't punish me when you are angry;
>   don't discipline me when you are furious.
> Have mercy on me, LORD,
>   because I'm frail.
> Heal me, LORD,
>   because my bones are shaking in terror!
> My whole body is completely terrified!
>   But you, LORD! How long will this last?"
>   (Psalm 6:1-3).

Prayer concerns for the week:

Day 1 Northern kings: 2 Kings 14:23-29 (Jeroboam II)**; 15:8-12** (Zechariah)**; 15:13-16** (Shallum)**; 15:17-22** (Menahem)**; 15:23-26** (Pekahiah)**; 15:27-31** (Pekah)**; 17; 18:9-12** (Hoshea)

Day 2 Southern kings: 2 Kings 15:1-7 (Azariah/ Uzziah)**; 2 Kings 15:32-38; 2 Kings 16; 2 King 18-20** (Hezekiah)

Day 3 Micah 1–7 (judgment on Samaria and Judah; social evils and wicked leaders denounced; peace and security through obedience, God challenges Israel)

Day 4 Isaiah 1–4 (wickedness of Judah, God's judgment)**; 6–8** (vision in the Temple, Immanuel)

Day 5 Isaiah 9–11 (righteous rule of messiah, repentant remnant of Israel)**; 28–30** (oracles against Ephraim and Judah, siege of Jerusalem)**; 32** (hope for the future)**; 36–37** (Jerusalem threatened, Hezekiah consults Isaiah)

Day 6 "The Word of the Lord" and "Marks of Obedient Community"

Day 7   Rest, pray, and attend class.

THE WORD OF THE LORD

Three events happened almost simultaneously—the death of Jeroboam II in Israel (746 BC); the death of Uzziah in Judah (742 BC); and the rise of the great soldier Tilglath-pileser III, nicknamed "Pul," in Assyria (745-727 BC). As Amos and Hosea had predicted, God was raising up an agent of punishment. Israel plummeted toward disaster, anarchy, and death.

Kings of Israel

The mood of stability was shattered when Jeroboam II died. His son Zechariah was assassinated after six months by Shallum, who in turn was murdered by the violent Menahem. This cruel monarch served ten years, sometimes slaughtering his own people (2 Kings 15:16), often fighting losing battles with Assyria. He took money, lots of money, from the rich who had profited so much during the glory days of Jeroboam II and gave it as tribute to Assyria (15:19-20). Menahem died, and his son Pekahiah ruled two years before he was killed by Pekah. Hold King Pekah in your memory, because he joined forces with King Rezin of Syria (Aram) and rebelled against Assyria. They tried to coerce Judah to join them, failed, then attacked Judah in an effort to depose the Davidic King Ahaz (734 BC) and put in power a sympathetic substitute. The whole episode was a last-gasp effort. King Tiglath-pileser III crushed Syria and Israel in 732 BC, put a puppet, Hoshea—who killed Pekah—in power, and began exiling the people of Israel. Hoshea paid tribute as a subservient but then foolishly rebelled. Samaria was pulverized in 722/721 BC.

Kings of Judah

Now the spotlight shifts. To get a fix on the Southern Kingdom, Judah, during the time of the prophets Micah and Isaiah, we need to focus on four kings. The line was cleanly father to son, all descendants of King David:

- Uzziah (783-742 BC), also called Azariah
- Jotham (ruled alone, 742-735 BC)
- Ahaz (735-715 BC)
- Hezekiah (715-687 BC)

Uzziah took over at age sixteen and quickly became an aggressive ruler who took advantage of the world power vacuum as did the corresponding king, Jeroboam II, in Israel. Uzziah expanded the borders eastward and southward as far as Solomon's old port of Elath on the Gulf of Aqaba. During Uzziah's forty-year rule, trade flourished; and as in Israel, the rich became powerful and the poor were squeezed.

Toward the end of his life, Uzziah became arrogant. He even tried to offer a sacrifice in the Temple, knowing that only priests had that privilege. He was struck down with leprosy and thereafter isolated to separate living quarters (2 Chronicles 26:16-21). Jotham, his son, was co-regent for eight years, then king for seven or eight more years. He continued the policies of his father.

But when Jotham's son Ahaz became king (2 Kings 16:1), the power structure of the Near East began to change. Tiglath-pileser

NOTES

III had turned Assyria into an awesome world power. Young King Ahaz was ill-prepared for international politics. He refused an appeal by Syria and Israel to join forces against Assyria (Syro-Ephraimite War). When they attacked, trying to coerce him to join their modest coalition, Ahaz pleaded to Assyria for help. Ahaz even sent the king of Assyria a present of silver and gold from the Temple. During the brief dispute with Syria and Israel, Ahaz lost soldiers and land. Edom picked off the outlying territory of Elath.

Assyria considered Ahaz a confused weakling.

Later, after Tiglath-pileser had demolished Damascus and wounded Israel (732 BC), Ahaz met with Tiglath-pileser in Damascus and then ordered the Temple priest, Uriah, to copy the altar that was in Damascus and build a replica right in Solomon's Temple at Jerusalem (2 Kings 16:10-16). Whereas, his father and grandfather had avoided most Baal worship, even destroying some of the high places, Ahaz, in his desperate plight, "didn't do what was right . . . , instead, he walked in the ways of Israel's kings. He even burned his own son alive" (16:2-3). All of Ahaz's efforts to get the gods to help him were futile. Judah quickly became a vassal state of Assyria.

Hezekiah, a son of Ahaz, became king upon Ahaz's death (715 BC) and ruled until 687 BC. On one hand, he purified worship in the Temple. He celebrated Passover with a pomp and gladness not seen since King Solomon's time (2 Chronicles 30:26). Hezekiah gave hospitality to refugees from Israel who were fleeing Assyria's wrath. He built the famous tunnel of Hezekiah to insure water for Jerusalem in the event of siege.

But, in an effort to win independence for Judah, Hezekiah listened to both Egypt and Babylon. He quit paying tribute to Assyria. When King Sargon II of Assyria died (705 BC), Hezekiah rebelled.

The new king, Sennacherib, quashed this modest rebellion with a vengeance. He captured forty-six Judean fortified cities, including Lachish, Judah's second largest city (2 Kings 18:14-16). He received all the gold and silver Hezekiah could strip from the Temple and the palace. Sennacherib claimed, in an official Assyrian inscription, that he had confined Hezekiah in Jerusalem "like a bird in a cage." He came right up to the walls of Jerusalem and laid siege in 701 BC.

Why do we care about these ancient kings? Because the God of the Bible works in history, weighing the nations in a balance. Because we cannot understand the prophets without knowing the social, political, and economic context in which they spoke. Because the insights God provided through the prophets in their day have relevance to our troubled times.

Micah

Micah came from Moresheth, a small farming village nestled in the Judean foothills twenty-five miles southwest of Jerusalem. Micah's village often was overrun by the armies that periodically raced up and down that natural highway to Egypt. Micah, like Amos, never lost his rural mindset. Unlike Amos, who spoke out in Samaria, Micah prophesied in his own capital, Jerusalem. With unsophisticated boldness and with blunt, straightforward, sometimes rough, language, he went to the city and denounced the establishment:

> "Hear, leaders of Jacob,
>   rulers of the house of Israel!
> Isn't it your job to know justice?—
> you who . . . tear the skin off [my people],
>   and the flesh off their bones" (Micah 3:1-2).

Micah's call to preach was not dramatic, but it was real:

> "But me! I am filled with power,
>   with the spirit of the LORD" (3:8).

The book begins with a courtroom scene of scathing denunciation for both Israel and Judah. The Lord is summoned as a witness and marches out of the Temple with huge strides. When God walks on the mountains, they melt. God, the witness, is asked, "Who is responsible for the crime of Jacob [Israel]? . . . of Judah?" (1:5). God's answer: The centers of power, the capitals, Samaria and Jerusalem. They represent the sin of a divided kingdom and the heart of idolatry. Then God the witness becomes God the judge and pronounces sentence: "I will make Samaria a heap of rubble in the open field" (1:6).

Then follows a lament, a funeral hymn, for Judah's future fall (1:8). In order to sing it properly, Micah puts on a simple loincloth and walks into Jerusalem, barefoot and naked, a sign of mourning. All the towns of Judah will soon weep and be stripped naked.

Specifically, what were the crimes Micah denounced? Government policies and taxes robbed the peasant farmers, forcing them to sell their land and become indentured servants. The rich and powerful landowners lay awake at night devising schemes to strip the children of promise of their inheritance (2:1-2).

The people didn't want to hear what Micah had to say; they preferred the lies of the false prophets. The priests taught only for a handsome fee. The prophets preached peace when they ate well but lashed out against those who didn't pay them (3:5). When they gave oracles, they remembered how their bread was buttered.

The sanctuary prophets were not shameless charlatans. They simply were so much a part of the sins of the society they couldn't see the plumb line of God. That's why they didn't speak out. That's why they resented the criticism.

The judges took bribes (3:11). Taking money from the working people, they built enormous monuments and public works in the city. Micah insisted all were built with blood money (3:10). The merchants and traders used "wicked scales" and "false weights," another way of cheating the poor (6:11). Lies, misrepresentation of goods, and false advertising were ways of thievery and deceit (6:12). What will happen to these greedy people? They will never be satisfied. Even when they eat, they will never have enough (6:14-15).

Idolatry was rampant. Micah claimed the people went to the high places of Baal and brought their false gods into the Temple.

NOTES

God's Case Against the People

In Micah 6, God enters the courtroom again. God wants the universe to know "the LORD has a lawsuit against his people" (6:2). The defense asks, Did God do wrong in freeing you from slavery, in giving you Moses, in saving you, time after time (6:3-5)?

Almost innocently, the people ask what they should bring to the Lord in appreciation (6:6). What about a massive offering?

In a mighty answer, the prophet tells exactly what the Lord requires. In a single sentence God states Amos's demand for justice, Hosea's appeal for faithfulness to the covenant, and Isaiah's plea for quiet faith:

> "He has told you, human one, what is good and
> what the LORD requires from you:
> to do justice, embrace faithful love,
> and to walk humbly with your God" (Micah 6:8).

Micah, perhaps more than any other prophet, gave the hard word about Jerusalem: God "will make you [Jerusalem] a sign of destruction, / your inhabitants an object of hissing!" (6:16). The time is soon coming when you can't trust a friend or a member of your own family (7:5-6).

The people will be led off into exile (1:16), and "Jerusalem will become piles of rubble" (3:12).

But Jerusalem, though sorely attacked in the Assyrian siege, did not fall in 701 BC. The prophecy was totally fulfilled under the Babylonians in 587 BC. In the end, Micah looks into the heart of God and knows that people one day will stream back to the mountain of Zion where God will judge fairly and where peace will rule (4:2). Micah prophesied, using the same words as Isaiah:

> "They will beat their swords into iron plows
> and their spears into pruning tools"
> (Micah 4:3; Isaiah 2:4).

Micah, from the grazing lands of Moresheth, thought of God as shepherd.

> "He will stand and shepherd his flock. . . .
> he will become one [the Lord] of peace" (5:4-5).

Isaiah

The Book of Isaiah appears first among the sixteen prophetic books in the Bible, not because Isaiah lived before Amos and Hosea but because the book is so large, so majestic. It covers more than two centuries of prophetic writings and rises to incomparable poetic and spiritual heights. The full range of prophetic teachings from the peace and prosperity of mid-eighth century through the Assyrian and Babylonian destructions, even beyond the Exile to mid-fifth century, falls within its pages. If we could preserve only one book of Hebrew prophecy, encompassing maximum spiritual richness, we would save the Book of Isaiah.

It appears that the book contains the work of more than one prophet. We will look now at Isaiah 1–39 as the writings primarily of eighth-century Isaiah of Jerusalem, sometimes referred to as First Isaiah. We will study the other chapters of Isaiah in a few sessions.

Isaiah was a nobleman, born and bred in Jerusalem, and may have been a priest. His prestige and influence gave him a powerful pulpit and access to the highest level of decision-making.

Isaiah's Call

Why do we hear the message (Isaiah 1–5) before we meet the messenger (Isaiah 6)? Why do we listen to Isaiah's prophecies before we hear of his call? Because the message is more important than the messenger.

King Uzziah, the power of Judah for four decades, had died (6:1). Isaiah went to the Temple—perhaps to grieve, perhaps to pray for Jotham, the new king who would rule in troubled times. The earthly Temple was transformed for Isaiah into the heavenly Temple of God. Suddenly it was filled with all the hosts of heaven.

The Holy One of Israel was present. Celestial sights and sounds filled the young man's mind (6:3). Isaiah went to the Temple to pray for the king and instead met the King of heaven. The tears of grief for Uzziah glistened with the ecstasy of Holy Presence.

Before God, who is not aware of sin? "I'm a man with unclean lips, and I live among a people with unclean lips" (6:5). The prophet needed purification before he became God's messenger. The searing coal from the altar touched his lips and signified divine absolution (6:6-7).

Why did Isaiah focus on his lips? Perhaps as a prophet he was aware of the power of the words of his mouth. Or perhaps his lips were being prepared for the message of prophecy. Then as if God were surrounded by the heavenly council of advisers, the question came to Isaiah, "Whom shall I send, and who will go for us?" And the young prophet replied, "I'm here; send me" (6:8). Isaiah was willing. It is not always so.

When have you heard the voice of God calling you?

How did you respond to this call?

Sadly, most readers stop at Isaiah's response. We don't like the words that follow. Neither did Isaiah. When he preached, the people would not listen. He would plead, but they would not repent. They would stop up their ears, put their hands over their eyes (6:10). For how long?

"Until cities lie ruined . . . and the land is left devastated" (6:11).

Not a happy prospect for a budding preacher. Interestingly, some scholars hold the view that Isaiah had his Temple experience after he had been preaching for a while, and that it came about because he found that no one was listening to his message.

Isaiah's Message

At first, during King Jotham's reign, a time of peace and prosperity, Isaiah sounded like Amos and Hosea. He indicted Judah for its rebellion:

> "I reared children; I raised them up,
>   and they turned against me" (Isaiah 1:2).

The prophet announced that the upper classes (of which he was a part) had become greedy, disregarding the needs and rights of the poor and the weak. Isaiah saw God's covenant with King David and Mount Zion as the base for his beliefs. He firmly believed that the king, the descendant of David, was under obligation to guarantee justice for those who were poor and without power.

As a part of nobility, Isaiah saw the failures close at hand. Spiritual leadership was lacking. Without such leadership, the people forgot who they were. They mixed worship of false gods with worship of Israel's God. God wanted nothing to do with their many offerings.

Early on, Isaiah warned of coming punishment. He discerned, with a prophet's eye, that the whole body was sick. So he said God had chosen an enemy nation to bring judgment on Judah.

The prophet never doubted the Assyrians were coming. Only wholesale repentance could save Judah. Isaiah delivers the warning; he also holds out the promise—God will save. Isaiah's most dramatic sermon on this subject was no speech at all, but rather was his son, named Shear-jashub, "The remaining few will return" (7:3, note). Some people "of the house of Jacob" will survive (10:20). A people shall be saved out of Assyria just as Israel was brought out of Egypt (11:16).

Ahaz

Then Ahaz became king. When threatened by the combined forces of King Rezin of Syria and King Pekah of Israel in the Syro-Ephraimitic War (734 BC), the young king was terror-stricken. He had forgotten the Lord. The heart of Ahaz "and the hearts of [his] people shook as the trees of a forest shake when there is a wind" (Isaiah 7:2).

Isaiah offered the frightened Ahaz assurance. Isaiah promised a sign: A son would soon be born whose name *Immanuel* meant "God is with us." Before he was old enough to know good from evil, Syria and Israel would disappear (7:10-17). Later, Christians would see Jesus Christ in that sign.

But Ahaz could not wait (2 Kings 16). He appealed to King Tiglath-pileser III for help and later went to meet the king in Damascus. Isaiah felt Ahaz made a bad mistake in calling for help from the king of Assyria. That move showed lack of trust. It put Judah in a political bed with a potential enemy.

DISCIPLE FAST TRACK

In 732 BC, Assyria ravaged Syria and severely curtailed the position of Samaria, occupying some of the Israelite provinces, and for the first time implemented the Assyrian policy of interchange of captive peoples.

Hezekiah

Undoubtedly, the prophet was pleased when Hezekiah purified the Temple, cleansing it of Ahaz's abomination. Hezekiah also removed many of the Baal "high places" from the countryside. Hezekiah gets high marks from the historians who compared him to David, saying, "There was no one like him among all of Judah's kings" (2 Kings 18:5). However, Isaiah was troubled when Hezekiah became restless.

People were complaining about paying tribute to Assyria.

Egypt encouraged the small states that lay between Egypt and Assyria, like Philistia and Judah, to rebel. Isaiah condemned these rebellious ideas by walking barefoot and naked for three years (Isaiah 20:1-4). When Assyria attacked the coast, Egypt pulled back, leaving the Philistines high and dry. Judah escaped for the moment.

But with the death of the Assyrian king Sargon II, the whole area erupted in revolution. The fledgling power in Babylon sent a delegation with letters and a gift to Hezekiah, who had been sick (39:1). Egypt, experiencing revival, sent envoys, trying to join forces. Hezekiah fortified the Jerusalem walls.

In an hour of decision, Isaiah counseled Hezekiah to stay out of the revolution. The new Assyrian king, Sennacherib, did not know he was to be the instrument of God's anger. But his armies crushed Babylon, swept down the coast to the Nile, and into Judah as far as Jerusalem.

Now Isaiah, who had predicted destruction, made a strange turn. When everyone else thought the end had come, he announced God would save Jerusalem. The Assyrian official, the Rabshakeh, taunted Hezekiah from outside the city walls (36:4-10). But Isaiah, when consulted by the king, gave unbelievable advice: "The LORD says this: Don't be afraid. . . . I'm about to mislead him [King Sennacherib], so when he hears a rumor, he'll go back to his own country. Then I'll have him cut down by the sword in his own land" (37:6-7; 2 Kings 19:6-7). Isaiah, who had preached earlier against the revolution, now staunchly refused capitulation—and for the same reason. Stand firm, and see the salvation of the Lord (Isaiah 37:33-35).

What happened? The accounts in Isaiah 37:36-38 and 2 Kings 19:35-37 are mysterious. A plague among the Assyrian soldiers? We don't know. No matter. God had intervened, and David's city was saved. Isaiah's prophecy was fulfilled. Unfortunately, later leaders would interpret that prophecy to mean Jerusalem never would, never could be destroyed.

Hope

The sin of the people was great, but the zeal of the Lord was greater. Isaiah, a "man with unclean lips," felt the fire of holy

40

cleansing. So would Judah someday, for the ultimate purpose of God's fire is not to destroy but to purify.

Judgment will burn like a holy fire, but that holy fire will ultimately save.

Salvation will come through a child. Typical of Isaiah, who saw God working through the Davidic monarchy, a child will be born, a son with all authority on his shoulders (9:6-7). He will be a shoot out of Jesse, David's father (11:1).

He will reunite the two kingdoms (11:13). In that day when "the wolf will live with the lamb" (11:6) and "there will be . . . endless peace" (9:7), the people will know and love God.

For the people of Judah, this vision of God's great and final victory gave hope even amid the lament of national collapse. For the Christian community, Isaiah's promise has been the messianic vision of a child born of Davidic ancestry, who is the Savior of the world.

MARKS OF OBEDIENT COMMUNITY

The community of faith remembers that God is loving but expects just dealings and compassionate caring. We understand that injustice or cruelty brings judgment and punishment. We know that punishment is complex, communal—often unfathomable—and yet real and awful. We know that, under God, our actions influence others and theirs affect us.

Think about the innocent. Why do they often get caught up in the web of other people's sins?

What are some steps your DISCIPLE FAST TRACK group can take to work toward correcting injustices in your community? How could punishment come? How could punishment come to a city? a country?

Sometimes the faith community can hear the words of the prophet, sometimes not. God never gives up. On God's behalf, Isaiah wooed, chastised, pleaded. Sometimes the faith community is able to respond, to repent, to return, to reclaim the heritage; sometimes not. Today, wearing a big sign or shouting "repent" seems ineffective. What are ways to help people turn toward God?

IF YOU WANT TO KNOW MORE

Look for some hymns based on Isaiah's words. Read them aloud or sing them.

Isaiah 13–27 and 34–35 are not included in daily assignments. You may want to read those chapters.

Mark of Obedient Community
The community of faith recognizes that obedience to God requires just actions and repents of its failure to respond to God's pleas for justice and righteousness.

> "Look among the nations and watch!
> Be astonished and stare
> because something is happening in your days
> that you wouldn't believe even if told."
> —Habakkuk 1:5

5 God Rules the World

OUR HUMAN CONDITION

Things don't make sense. Evil seems rampant. There is talk of spiritual and moral decline. Warnings to "change or else" keep coming our way. But things are going nicely. Why change? It won't happen to us. Or, do we have false confidence? Are we misreading the signs? Is this God's plan?

ASSIGNMENT

These three prophets (Zephaniah, Nahum, Habakkuk) are among the twelve "minor" or "latter" prophets—"minor" because they are short (not unimportant), "latter" because they appear last (not least). Each book has its own unique message. Jeremiah's ministry is long, his prophetic work varied, his emotional life interwoven with Judah.

Events in the book flow neither sequentially nor smoothly. Stop from time to time to ponder what you are dealing with. Notice how reluctantly, how painfully Jeremiah spoke. See how lonely he was. Savor his imagery.

CONTEXT

Who
Zephaniah, Nahum, Habakkuk, and Jeremiah

Where
The Southern Kingdom

When
From King Manasseh's reign (687 BC), through King Josiah's reign and reform (640-609 BC), and almost to the fall of the Jerusalem (586 BC).

Condition of the People
From 687 to 642 BC Judah is ruled by evil King Manasseh. He reverses all of King Hezekiah's religious reforms. Life is peaceful, but people are moving further and further away from God.

Around 640 BC, King Josiah begins religious reform. But in 609 BC, Josiah is killed in battle. Religious reform ends. Kings who do "evil in the eyes of the LORD" rule in Judah. Kings after Josiah are put into power either by election of the people or by one of the great powers (first Egypt, then Babylon). The death of Josiah creates a theological crisis since his reforms should have brought blessing to the people.

In the nearby region, in 612 BC, Babylon conquers Assyria and begins taking over the massive Assyrian Empire. Twenty-six years later, in 586 BC, Babylon conquers and destroys the Southern Kingdom, Jerusalem, and the Temple. Almost all are slaughtered or led into exile.

Main Message
Zephaniah: Prophet during the religious reform of King Josiah. *Message:* Time has run out. You have one last chance to repent. If not, God will destroy the nation. But even after the destruction, God will bring up a new generation devoted to him.

Nahum: Prophet before the fall of Assyria. *Message:* All nations are under divine judgment. Though Assyria is the enemy of Israel, and thus the enemy of Israel's God, God has allowed Assyria free reign with Israel for a time in order to judge the people of God. But eventually God will reassert God's goodness and power. God's people will be restored while Assyria will fall. And, Assyria does fall in 612 BC when conquered by the Babylonians.

Habakkuk: Prophet between the fall of Assyria to Babylon, and the fall of Jerusalem to Babylon. *Message:* In bad times, even when it seems like God is doing nothing to help, trust in God.

Jeremiah: Prophet before, during, and after the fall of the Southern Kingdom in 586 BC. *Message:* Punishment is coming due to Judah's long history of sinning. God will allow Judah to be destroyed by other nations and to be exiled.

Prayer
Pray daily before study:

> "I was thrown on you from birth;
>   you've been my God
>   since I was in my mother's womb.
> Please don't be far from me,
> because trouble is near
>   and there's no one to help"
>   (Psalm 22:10-11).

Prayer concerns for the week:

Day 1 Zephaniah 1–3 (coming day of the Lord, judgment on Judah and on Israel's enemies, a righteous remnant)**; Nahum 1–3** (oracle of the destruction of Nineveh)

Day 2 Habakkuk 1–3 (Habakkuk and God in dialogue. Habakkuk's prayer)**; 2 Chronicles 33:1–36:10** (Manasseh, Amon, Josiah and the Instruction scroll)

Day 3 Jeremiah 1–3 (Jeremiah's call, Israel's apostasy, call to repent)**; Jeremiah 4–6** (a doomed nation, invasion and desolation of Judah coming)

Day 4 Jeremiah 7:1–29 (Temple sermon)**; 11–13** (broken covenant, linen undergarment, wine jug, threat of captivity)

Day 5 Jeremiah 16–20 (sin of Judah, the potter and the clay, Sabbath, personal laments, the broken jar)

Day 6 "The Word of the Lord" and "Marks of Obedient Community"

Day 7 Rest, pray, and attend class.

THE WORD OF THE LORD

Zephaniah: Judgment

Zephaniah, a descendant of David, moved about easily with leaders of government in Jerusalem (Zephaniah 1:10-11). He began prophesying sometime after 640 BC when Josiah became king of Judah. Josiah was only eight years old, and Zephaniah may have been part of a group of reformers who tutored the young king and prayed for religious revival.

For nearly half a century, Judah had been ruled by King Manasseh (687-642 BC). From a secular viewpoint, the times were not too bad. After the siege of 701 BC was lifted, Judah lived as a vassal state under an imposed Assyrian peace. Life in the villages normalized; trade in the city prospered. Though the people of Judah paid an enormous tribute, at least the wars had stopped. But from a religious viewpoint, life was a disaster. Manasseh undid all of his father Hezekiah's reforms. In an effort to appease Assyria, Judah imported all sorts of foreign gods.

Zephaniah pointed to three great sins nurtured by Manasseh and his son Amon (642-640 BC)—idolatry, syncretism (the mixing and intermingling of all kinds of religion), and indifference. Perhaps this third sin was the worst. God was irrelevant. Zephaniah pictures God with lamps, walking the streets of Jerusalem, looking for people who ignored God's rule. What God found was complacency, like wine left too long with the sediment (1:12).

Zephaniah knew Judah was supposed to be distinct, different, a people set apart (Exodus 33:16; Numbers 23:9). But King Manasseh was practical, compromising, accommodating.

The Bible says King Manasseh not only served the longest as king but was the worst king in Judah's history (2 Kings 21:1-9). The first sixty years of the seventh century BC were a religious wasteland. No prophet is recorded to have spoken in Judah since Micah and Isaiah.

Now, according to Zephaniah, God was angry. All the nations, including Judah, were condemned. Sin had infected all nature, even the animals, the birds, and the fish of the sea. Judgment would begin in Jerusalem, then spread throughout the world (Zephaniah 1:4, 18).

Around 620 BC, Josiah, now in his twenties, began a religious reform (2 Kings 23). He renovated the Temple. In the process, the high priest Hilkiah found a portion of the Book of Deuteronomy, "the Instruction scroll" (22:8). Josiah had the scroll read aloud and proceeded to enforce it. He purified the Temple, tore down the "high places," defiled the place of child sacrifice, and celebrated Passover throughout the kingdom. Zephaniah pleaded for massive repentance:

> "Seek righteousness;
> seek humility.
> Maybe you will be hidden on the day of the
>   LORD's anger" (Zephaniah 2:3).

But Egypt's armies swept up the coast and met Judah's army. Josiah was mortally wounded and died shortly after in Jerusalem (2 Kings 23:29; 2 Chronicles 35:20-24), resulting in Judah's becoming a vassal of Egypt. Josiah, high hope of Zephaniah (and Jeremiah), was dead.

Zephaniah despaired. He realized the people's deep pride:

> "She [Jerusalem] listened to no voice;
>   she has accepted no discipline.
> She didn't trust in the LORD,
>   nor did she draw near to her God" (Zephaniah 3:2).

The prophet condemned four groups of people—princes who devour the poor, judges who steal, prophets who are frivolous windbags, and priests who ignore Torah. People are not even ashamed (3:3-5). The prophet's call for repentance has gone unheeded. The reform is superficial, not a real conversion of the heart.

Zephaniah's theme is the sin of human pride (3:11). People believe they can control the world and their own destiny without God and God's ways.

The faithful will recognize that God, not they, controls the world. How do you see people today trying to control the world and their own destiny without God and God's ways?

Nahum: Destruction of Nineveh

Nahum's two poems concentrate on a single message: God will bring judgment on Nineveh. In vivid detail, Nahum foretells the destruction of Nineveh. *Egypt*

The people of Judah were not alone in celebrating Assyria's collapse, but they were front and center among the cheerleaders. They had suffered much; so had the Medes, the Egyptians, the Scythians, and the Babylonians. All joined in the victory shout.

Remember this slice of history: Assyria's day in the sun was crowded with cruelty. Its fierce armies raged across the desert to burn, pillage, and rape. At the height of its power, Assyria ruled the area from the plateaus of northern Iran to the upper reaches of the Nile, an expanse of over a thousand miles.

Assyria went to great lengths to use terror as an instrument of public policy. They believed fear would melt opposition, that terror would bring about passive submission. Their custom was to inflict unnecessary pain. But these strategies had the reverse effect. Intense hatred burned in the hearts of subject peoples all over the empire.

The Word in Nahum

Can we discern the word from the Lord in Nahum? Consider:

God allows all manner of human emotions to be expressed. The Bible contains raw humanness, flesh-and-blood reality. People who are angry say so. What could be more human than for Judah to celebrate freedom from oppression, to rejoice in the possibilities of peace once again?

God holds evil on a tether. God will not let wickedness run rampant forever. God gets weary of evil regimes and calls them to accountability.

Most of the Hebrew prophets condemned the sins of Israel and Judah and foretold awful consequences. Nahum reminds us that all nations are under divine judgment, that evil will not go undisciplined forever. Just because Assyria served for a time as the instrument of God's wrath, that does not mean Assyria will go unpunished for its gross cruelties.

Nahum seems not to see the Babylonian invasion looming in the not-too-distant future. He fails to provide the call to repentance that might restore Judah to wholeness. Still he expresses a shout of victory, for God has acted.

Habakkuk: In God's Time

Little or nothing is known about the prophet Habakkuk, except that he prophesied in Judah toward the end of King Josiah's reign. He may have seen reform come to a halt with Josiah's death (609 BC). He may even have learned of the great battle when Egypt's upward reaches were smashed by Babylonia at Carchemish (605 BC). Judah's dreams of independence were shattered. Babylon would soon rule the world.

So Habakkuk began to question God. "LORD, how long will I cry for help . . . ?" (Habakkuk 1:2). Trouble continued.

Strife and violence were everywhere. Justice did not prevail. Order was slipping into chaos (1:2-4).

Habakkuk's question is not, Is there a God? Nor is the question, Is God just? The question is about the providence of God. Is God really making any progress toward achieving God's ultimate plan of order, justice, and peace? God answers in effect, "I'm not asleep. Look, I'm doing great things." God is doing a work so mighty that Habakkuk wouldn't believe it even if he were told. Then God lets the prophet in on a terrible secret. God is "about to rouse the Chaldeans," the Babylonians (1:6). They are fierce and terrible. They will destroy the Assyrians who have cruelly ruled the world for more than two hundred years.

Habakkuk is bewildered, horrified. Lord, "your eyes are too pure to look on evil" (1:13). The Babylonians are "treacherous."

God responds, in effect, "I'm going to explain the matter so clearly you can write it on a billboard. The dream that chaos will become order—the vision that nation will not lift up sword against nation, the goal of a time of justice and peace—is not lost. God is ushering in the great day of harmony. "If it delays, wait for it" (2:3). Be patient. There is still a vision for the appointed time. As

NOTES

a person of faith, Habakkuk, you are living in the "not yet," in the "meanwhile" times of faith and trust. The righteous will live, quietly, humbly, trusting God in faithfulness (2:4).

God sets a limit on human wickedness. The proud challengers of God's rule cannot *rest* or *abide* or *live* (2:4-5). God is working out God's purpose.

Is there still a vision? As Habakkuk prays, he stands in awe (3:2), remembering God's power in the past and praying for God's activity in the present. Habakkuk is given a vision of God's ultimate purpose fulfilled. God will come again to conquer the chaos just as at the time of Creation.

No more questions rise to the prophet's lips; no more anguish disturbs his peace. God is working out the vision. For us, in the interim, we are to live out the instruction, "the righteous live [now and forever] by their faith" (2:4, NRSV).

Think of a time in your life when you didn't feel like God was answering your prayers at all or in the way you wanted. What response to God did you have? Were you able to trust God no matter what? Explain.

Jeremiah

Jeremiah was born shortly after the child Josiah was made king of Judah. Jeremiah's father and some of his family were priests in the village of Anathoth, situated a few miles northeast of Jerusalem. Perhaps Jeremiah was a descendant of Abiathar, the high priest banished to Anathoth by King Solomon for political reasons (1 Kings 2:26-27).

We can identify four phases in Jeremiah's ministry. His early ministry lasted from his call (626 BC) to the discovery of "the Instruction scroll" (the scroll of Deuteronomy) (622 BC). The second phase was a time of pulling back from public life as the prophet anxiously watched the reform movement unfold. The third phase, during the reign of Jehoiakim (609-598 BC), was a time of spiritual crisis when Jeremiah became vigorously active again, much as Isaiah had done during the rule of Hezekiah. His final phase of ministry coincided with Zedekiah and the Exile (597-587 BC).

God's Call

No call is formed in a vacuum. Did Jeremiah's mother put drops of honey on the Torah scrolls when he was a child so he would love the Scriptures? Did his father, a village priest in Anathoth, take him by the hand when they walked from the village to the Temple, three or four miles away? How did the boy know that God loves an honest measure, hates a bribe, and cares for the poor? He must have learned it at home.

Jeremiah's call from God was overwhelming.

DISCIPLE FAST TRACK

"Before I created you in the womb I knew you;
  before you were born I set you apart" (Jeremiah 1:5).

Then visions came—an almond branch (God will perform his word) and a boiling pot, tilted from the north (Babylon is coming). The message was the vision; the vision was the call; and the call, etched deeply in his mind, became a fire in his bones (20:9). Jeremiah prophesied in Judah for nearly half a century (626-580 BC) during his country's most frightening and tragic period of history.

Jeremiah announced a message that ran contrary to his own natural inclinations. Deep inside, he would have preferred to have spoken differently. He cared enormously about his people but was driven against his nature by a holy word that had to be spoken.

Beginning Ministry

Much of Jeremiah's early work is recorded in Jeremiah 1–6. We can hear in his preaching the influence of earlier prophets. Like Amos and Micah, he denounced greed. Following Hosea, Jeremiah understood faith as a love relationship as well as obedience to the Law. Like Hosea, he used both the father-son and the husband-wife analogies to reflect the intimacy between the Lord and Israel. Just like Hosea, Jeremiah denounced the nation's spiritual harlotry.

Jeremiah was filled with despair over the moral and spiritual decline he witnessed. Some prophets only chastised the leaders, but Jeremiah lambasted the entire population—rich and poor, high and low.

More than any other prophet, Jeremiah cries out for repentance, for a radical return. "'Return, faithless people,' declares the LORD, 'for I am your husband' " (3:14, NIV). It is the heart of the people that is evil. The heart must be changed. Circumcision, the ancient rite every male child received as a sign of identification with the covenant people, is not enough.

As Jeremiah grew older, he, like Isaiah, realized the people's ears were closed and their eyes were shut (5:21).

The problem of idolatry is pride, a pride that confuses the creation with the Creator, that sees this world as an end in itself. That pride links politics and economics into an oppressive form, fortified by a religion of false gods that are under official control. Jeremiah believed God was trying to get the people to grieve, to weep, to change before it was too late.

King Josiah's Reform

Josiah, even as a teenager, began to reverse the religious syncretism (mixing pagan gods with worship of Israel's one God) of his father Amon and his grandfather Manasseh. Perhaps he was tutored by priests and prophets zealous for the Lord. But he was also supported by nationalistic zealots who sensed the power vacuum in Mesopotamia as Assyria began to falter. So Josiah began to repair the Temple in Jerusalem.

That act was perceived by Assyria as rebellion.

King Josiah had a twofold vision—religiously to purify Jewish ritual leading to Deuteronomic reform (2 Kings 23:21-24) and politically to reunite the divided kingdoms under one king of Davidic descent. Probably the single most important aspect of Josiah's reform was the centralization of worship in Jerusalem—one God, one people, one form of worship. Without doubt, every act of Josiah, religious or otherwise, was seen by Assyria as sedition and rebellion. Fortunately for Judah, Assyria was too weak to respond. Unfortunately for Judah, both Egypt and Babylon were moving into the power vacuum. The whole nation of Judah, religious leaders and national patriots, wept when Josiah was killed (609 BC). Jeremiah wrote a lament to express his own and the nation's grief (2 Chronicles 35:25).

Memory

Prophets lifted up the core memory:

"The Lord proclaims:
Stop at the crossroads and look around;
    ask for the ancient paths.
Where is the good way?
Then walk in it
    and find a resting place for yourselves" (Jeremiah 6:16).

The prophets called for people to believe and practice what they already knew. "Israel, listen! Our God is the Lord! Only the Lord! Love the Lord your God with all your heart, all your being, and all your strength" (Deuteronomy 6:4-5). Judah tested her prophets by whether their foretelling actually came true. Jeremiah said often that after the destruction came, the people would know who were the false prophets and who the true prophets. Centuries later we read Jeremiah's words, and we soberly say, "It came to pass."

During the reign of King Jehoiakim, Jeremiah denounced the people for their belief that God would protect the Temple and them. He walked boldly into the Temple courtyard on a holy festival day. Judeans were there from all over the world. Jeremiah shouted his sermon at the crowd: "Don't trust in lies: 'This is the Lord's temple! The Lord's temple! The Lord's temple!'" (7:4).

They misunderstood the meaning of Shiloh, said Jeremiah. Shiloh, about sixteen miles north of Jerusalem, was the most important place of worship during the period of the judges. The ark of the covenant had rested there. Hannah, Samuel's mother, had prayed there. Eli taught young Samuel at Shiloh. It was Saul's favorite sanctuary, but the Philistines destroyed it. Now the people of Judah said, Aha, that meant God wanted the place of supreme worship to be in David's city, in the Temple in Jerusalem. God will protect his house forever.

Jeremiah said, You've got it all wrong. The same God who permitted Shiloh to be destroyed will allow Jerusalem to be destroyed also. You are violating Torah so badly, fracturing covenant so completely, that God will allow the Babylonians to ravage your Temple. You are putting your trust in the Temple, not in God. Worship for you has become mechanical. You practice wickedness; you worship as hypocrites. Then you boast that the holy God of Israel will protect you from all enemies. You are deceiving yourselves.

When Jeremiah denounced the Temple, the priests, the prophets, and even the people wanted to kill him. What saved him was the historic tradition that allowed unpopular prophets to speak. "A few of the community elders got up and addressed the whole crowd: 'Micah of Moresheth, who prophesied during the rule of Judah's Hezekiah, said . . . "Jerusalem will become piles of rubble"'" (Jeremiah 26:17-18). Micah's prophecy and Judah's tolerance saved Jeremiah's life.

But Jeremiah became weary. Everyone was turning against him. He complained to God. God's answer was tough:

> "If you have raced people and you are worn out,
>   how will you compete with horses?" (12:5).

Recall times when you thought you were spiritually exhausted, only to discover that more difficult challenges still lay ahead.

Don't miss the imagery of Jeremiah and the crashing clay jar (Jeremiah 19:1-13). He breaks it with great ceremony. Jerusalem would be so broken. That act put him in stocks where people could walk by, laugh at him, and mock him (20:2, 7). The broken jar sermon and the punishment that followed caused Jeremiah to reconsider his divine call. Had not God told him in that early teenage call,

> "'Don't be afraid of them,
> because I'm with you to rescue you,'
>   declares the LORD" (1:8)?

The prophet wished he had never been born (20:14), but the searing sense of call would not go away.

> "There's an intense fire in my heart,
>   trapped in my bones" (20:9).

The reconsideration is over. The message is a part of him. Sometimes we have to do something because we think it right. No way to get out of it whatever the cost.

When, if ever, have you felt that way?

MARKS OF OBEDIENT COMMUNITY

The faith community is at home in the "meantime" because it remembers and is confident that God is at work in ways we can't imagine. In God's time we will see the working out of God's purposes. Toward that end we respond to God's call to repent.

Are you ever tempted to doubt that God is in control? If so, say why.

Mark of Obedient Community
The obeying community weeps over a broken, unheeding world, repents of its actions that contradict God's purposes, and is confident that God is ultimately in control.

For what do we most need to repent—false gods? blending our gods with our God? indifference?

IF YOU WANT TO KNOW MORE

Israel and Judah were often forced to pay tribute to foreign nations. Look up *tribute* in a Bible dictionary.

See what you can discover about kings Esar-haddon, Ashurbanipal, Nabopolassar, and the city of Carchemish.

"I regard them as good, and I will bring them back to this land. I will build them up and not pull them down; I will plant them and not dig them up. I will give them a heart to know me, for I am the LORD. They will be my people, and I will be their God, for they will return to me with all their heart."

—Jeremiah 24:6-7

6 God Will Not Abandon

OUR HUMAN CONDITION

We prefer to hear positive things even if they are false. Though our families and our communities may be falling apart, we ignore the warning signs and reject the messages we don't like.

ASSIGNMENT

Read Jeremiah 22–26 before 21 to help you keep the kings in order. (Chapter 21 is out of sequence.) Why did the editors of the Jeremiah materials put the Jehoiakim scroll incident (Jeremiah 36) out of place and after much Zedekiah material? Because it graphically symbolizes Jeremiah's entire ministry and Judah's consistent response. Make notes as you read to keep straight in your mind who the various kings are and where they fit into history. Remember three—good Josiah, bad Jehoiakim, and weak Zedekiah.

CONTEXT

Who
Jeremiah

Where
Southern Kingdom, Judah

When
609-580 BC. After King Josiah's death through the fall of Jerusalem.

Condition of the People
Life is full of godless kings, who do evil in the sight of God. There is no religious reform. Babylon is striking closer and closer. Some are taken into exile. Kings are changing. Things are unstable. But some are still living in wealth and denial. Idols are worshiped. The wealthy still take advantage of the poor.

Main Message
Jeremiah: He pleads for repentance. Jeremiah speaks truth of coming devastation. Jeremiah announces that after seventy years of exile, God is going to bring back a remnant of the faithful to Jerusalem. He proclaims God's new covenant with the people.

PRAYER

Pray daily before study:

"Tell me all about your faithful love come morning time,
    because I trust you.
Show me the way I should go,
    because I offer my life up to you"
                    (Psalm 143:8).

Prayer concerns for the week:

NEW COVENANT

Day 1 Jeremiah 22–26 (royal arrogance, Branch of David, false prophets, good and bad figs, captivity foretold, Temple sermon)**; 2 Kings 23:31–24:19** (Jehoahaz [Shallum], Jehoiakim, Jehoiachin, Zedekiah)

Day 2 Jeremiah 21; 27–29 (oracle against Jerusalem, the yoke, Hananiah opposes Jeremiah, letter to the exiles, Shemaiah)**; 2 Chronicles 36:11-21** (Zedekiah)

Day 3 Jeremiah 30–33 (promised return, a new covenant, Jeremiah buys a field, the righteous Branch)

Day 4 Jeremiah 34–36 (slaves freed, sign of the Rechabites, the scroll read and burned)**; 2 Kings 25** (siege of Jerusalem, Judah in captivity)

Day 5 Jeremiah 37–38 (Jeremiah imprisoned, consultations with Zedekiah)**; 42:7–44:14** ("Do not go to Egypt," Jeremiah taken to Egypt)**; 52** (destruction reviewed)

Day 6 "The Word of the Lord" and "Marks of Obedient Community"

Day 7 Rest, pray, and attend class.

DISCIPLE FAST TRACK

THE WORD OF THE LORD

Jeremiah was a voice to be reckoned with. No matter what the kings did or what the court prophets said, they looked at Jeremiah out of the corner of their eyes. He had access to the kings, and he constantly demanded justice. If the kings would turn and be faithful to their duty to do justice, the Davidic dynasty could continue; if not, other nations would wonder why the Lord punished Judah so severely.

Jehoiakim

Some leaders of Judah wished good King Josiah could return. They still mourned. Jeremiah said, Don't weep for him; weep for Jehoahaz (Shallum), who will never come back from Egypt (Jeremiah 22:10). Now comes the frontal attack on Jehoiakim. In Judah's most critical hour, the arrogant king remodeled his quarters. He used the most expensive materials, imported woods and furnishings. Lacking money, he conscripted poor working people, families off their plots of land, and made them work without pay (22:13-17).

What an act of *self-deception*! That beautiful mansion would soon smolder in ashes. What an example of *injustice*! Conscripted labor would cause families to go hungry, farmers to lose their crops, laborers to become slaves. What an illustration of *arrogance*, of pride, of trusting self! Remember, the prophet Micah had declared a king's job was to do justice and to provide equity (Micah 3:9-10). From the beginning, kings of Israel were to serve, not to be served.

Do you call yourself a king because you excel in remodeling? Don't miss the key word the prophet uses, *countrymen*: The king works "his countrymen for nothing" (Jeremiah 22:13). Jews in the covenant community were to eat manna together, to be free, to be neighbors, from the least to the greatest.

Jeremiah appealed to the memory of the king's father, Josiah, who "defended the rights of the poor and needy" (22:16). Then it was well in the land. But the appeal failed.

Jeremiah forecast the lonely burial: No one will call Jehoiakim "brother"; no one will mourn, saying, "My master, my majesty!" (22:18). He will be buried without fuss or bother, like a dead farm animal (22:19). Jehoiakim died when he was about thirty-six years of age, during the siege of Jerusalem. His son Jehoiachin, called "Coniah" in 22:24, would soon be carried to Babylon where he would die. Nothing could stop the inevitable. God would cast him away even if he were "the signet ring" on God's right hand (22:24). "Mark this man as childless," said Jeremiah, for no descendant of Jehoiachin would sit on David's throne (22:30).

The prophet enlarged the concept of "shepherds" (23:1-4). Not only the king but the leaders of the nation, including priests and prophets, were supposed to be "shepherds." Instead, the leaders were destroying and scattering the sheep (23:1).

In our nation, in our towns, in our churches, how are our leaders self-serving? Or how are they shepherds?

Because the leaders have failed, God will step in personally after the "scattering" takes place to be shepherd for Israel, just as in the beginning (23:3). A glimmer of hope begins to shine in Jeremiah. Someday, after the destruction, after the Exile, God will bring the lost sheep of Israel back into the fold. A righteous king will rule (23:5). No longer will the people of Israel refer to the Lord as the one who brought them up out of the land of Egypt; after the ingathering they will say, the Lord who brought us back out of the lands of captivity (23:7-8).

Jeremiah blasts the court prophets, calling them "adulterers" (23:9-17). The term likely meant an "adulterous" relationship with other gods from foreign lands, thereby making them spiritually unfaithful. They were liars. They aided those in power who were destroying the country.

Without question the great prophets of Israel and Judah expected moral and spiritual leadership from those with political and religious authority. How much of that expectation do we still have? In what sense is it appropriate for us to expect a lot? How are our leaders measuring up?

The vision of the good figs and the bad figs (Jeremiah 24) carries a simple message. The good figs are those exiles carried into Babylon by the earlier invasion. The bad figs are those people remaining in Jerusalem, still resisting God's will. Once again Jeremiah runs at cross purposes with the court prophets. They were smugly saying that God had punished the wicked by removing them, that God had rewarded the righteous by allowing them to remain. Just the opposite, said Jeremiah. Those who are still rebellious will die (24:8-10); those who have been deported will return (24:5-7).

From a purely historical viewpoint, years later the Jews who came home to rebuild were those who had been disciplined by years in exile. They came rejoicing with new zeal and fresh spiritual insight. Most of the postexilic writings, most of the theological editing of Deuteronomy, Kings, and Chronicles came from the pens of these Jews of the Diaspora. Jeremiah is specific now (25). King Nebuchadnezzar is God's servant for a time, an agent of punishment for Judah and surrounding nations. His own punishment will come later, after a decade of sabbaths, about seventy years. God rules all the nations of the world.

Public Debate

Our sympathies go out to King Zedekiah. He was in a tough spot. True, the Babylonians had put him in power after their invasion of 598. But now Babylon was having troubles in other parts of the empire. Egypt offered to join Judah in armed rebellion. Many politicians and most of the prophets were saying, "Strike now; it is time to be free. God is with us." To think otherwise was to appear pro-Babylonian and traitorous to Temple and king.

King Zedekiah had already joined forces with Egypt in rebellion against Babylon before he called Jeremiah in for advice (Jeremiah 21:1-2). Perhaps the prophet would give consolation even as Isaiah had been able to do for Hezekiah a century before. But to no avail. Jeremiah's eye was single. The enemy was God, and Babylon at this moment was doing God's bidding. Stop the rebellion, yield to the Babylonians (Chaldeans). Those words during wartime smacked of cowardice and complicity. Zedekiah ignored them.

Symbolic Yoke

Jeremiah built a symbolic yoke of straps and bars (wood), similar to the yoke used on oxen (Jeremiah 27:2). He put it on his shoulders and apparently wore it around town to send a message: God put the yoke of Babylon on Judah and other nations. Everyone, including the prophet Hananiah, was saying the exiles would soon be free and would bring the precious silver and gold Temple vessels back home (28:2-3). Watch carefully in Jeremiah 28:6-9; Jeremiah responds somewhat respectfully, in effect, "Amen; so be it." That would be wonderful. But those prophets who preceded you and me told of war and not of peace. If peace comes, you will be right. But it will not come. Hananiah tore off Jeremiah's yoke right in the Temple courtyard (28:10). He shouted that God would break the yoke that Babylon was forcing them to wear and the exiles would soon be home.

Jeremiah's vision was still crystal clear. He announced that a heavier yoke was coming, a yoke forged of iron bars. And he said Hananiah did not have the word of the Lord. In fact, within the year, Hananiah would be dead because he had "incited rebellion against the LORD." Two months later, Hananiah died (28:16-17).

Correspondence moved back and forth between Jerusalem and the exiles from 598 to 590. Jeremiah wrote, "Get married and have children; then help your sons find wives and your daughters find husbands in order that they too may have children. Increase in number there so that you do not dwindle away. Promote the welfare of the city where I have sent you into exile. Pray to the LORD for it, because your future depends on its welfare" (29:6-7). Jeremiah saw the hand of God working out a slow but important providential design. The Jews in the Diaspora would learn that God is not just the God of favored Israel but God of the nations, not limited to Jerusalem but living in all the world. Jeremiah also knew that, tempered and sobered, they would be the remnant people to whom God would give a new covenant (31:31-34).

NOTES

Shemaiah, one of the false prophets, wrote an angry letter back asking the Temple authorities to shut Jeremiah up, for he was taking the heart out of the exiles (29:24-28). They thought their thin thread of hope lay in the salvation of the Temple and in a quick return. Jeremiah knew their only hope lay in the God of the universe who would sustain them if they would trust.

Restoration sometimes takes a long time. That's why faith is essential. Contemplate a time of exile for you, your family, or your country when restoration was a long time coming.

When you find it hard to wait on the Lord, what helps you?

How do you know when to act and when to wait?

A New Covenant

Mostly, Jeremiah is not apocalyptic in the sense of seeing a vision of end times, of a new world to come. Rather, he sees the exiles returning to the land of Judah, renewed in spirit. They will come back to the land of promise. The assurance is clear. The Babylonian yoke will one day be broken by the Lord (Jeremiah 30:8).

The entire experience of exile was an act of divine discipline. God punished Israel as a loving parent corrects a child. God not only will punish but will teach as well. The prophet warned Israel to "set up markers" so they would learn from this experience (31:21). So their geographical return home would also be a return by way of Torah to faithfulness. Then came a theological breakthrough. We will spot it again in Ezekiel. People were saying, we're suffering because of our parents' sins (they ate sour grapes, so our teeth are set on edge). There was truth in that, of course. But a bold new truth was emerging. We don't have to suffer for the sins of our ancestors. We can be freed from that to wrestle with our own problems (31:29-30). In other words, we can't blame our parents; we are responsible for our own predicament.

God will make a new covenant with Israel (31:31-34) to replace their earlier covenant with God, broken through their disobedience. The renewed people in a new covenant will have faithful and obedient hearts for God.

Time for Hope

Jeremiah languished in prison, listening to the sounds of war. A cousin named Hanamel appeared, just as God had said he would, wanting to sell a family property in Anathoth, a few miles away in already-occupied territory (Jeremiah 32:6-15). The grapevines had been torn down, the booth arbors burned, and the destitute cousin wanted Jeremiah to buy the land so the family would not lose it. Since Jeremiah was next of kin, he had first right of purchase to protect the family inheritance (Leviticus 25:25-31).

Instead of laughing at the ludicrous proposal, Jeremiah knew God was speaking once again. While he sat in the court of the guard, wondering how to give hope to Judah, God sent him a cousin with a farm to sell! Jeremiah took infinite pains to make everything legal (and to dramatize the symbolic act). They transferred cash (the full value of the land in peacetime) and signed the deeds. Witnesses watched the transaction. Jeremiah instructed Baruch, his secretary, to make a public filing of the deeds and to deposit them where they would be safe (Jeremiah 32:14).

The word went out that Jeremiah believed God would bring the people home and one day people would farm the land again. The word has gone out across the centuries that in the moment of deepest despair God does not abandon God's people.

When have you experienced someone acting with hope in a moment of despair, giving encouragement to others?

Jeremiah Rejected

Picture the prophet, barred from the Temple and the palace, working with his scribe and friend Baruch, preparing a scroll of prophecy for the people of Judah and the king (36:1-8). Watch King Jehoiakim as Jehudi reads the message aloud in the king's private chamber. After hearing each portion, Jehoiakim, unaffected by what he has heard, takes his penknife, cuts off the passage from the scroll, and throws that piece into the fire (36:21-23). What a graphic portrayal of total rejection. Jeremiah learns about the incident, as does all of Judah. He and Baruch prepare a second scroll with much of the same material. The climax of the incident comes in 36:31: "I will punish him [Jehoiakim] and his family. . . . I will bring upon . . . the people of Judah, every disaster I pronounced against them. But they wouldn't listen."

Taken to Egypt

After the collapse of the city, the Babylonians offered to take care of Jeremiah in Babylon, but he chose to stay among the people in the land (Jeremiah 40:2-6). In response to an inquiry from the people, Jeremiah counseled them and their leaders not to seek haven in Egypt but to stay as a remnant in Judah. His counsel was rejected. Then some of his enemies took him and Baruch along with others and carried them to Egypt. What could be a more fitting symbol than to be taken unwillingly to Egypt? Jeremiah's last recorded words were of ruin for Egypt and of the consequences of the choice to leave Judah and, in effect, Judah's God and the covenant. Thus, Baruch and Jeremiah became Jews of the Diaspora.

Jeremiah never lost the fire in his bones, never lost faith that God is in ultimate control. He died in Egypt, still owning land in Judah where one day, as he had foretold, people would return, raise their children and their crops, and "know the LORD."

MARKS OF OBEDIENT COMMUNITY

We want to listen to the word of the Lord speaking to us today. What is tearing at the fabric of our homes? our communities? What can we do about it?

The prophets, no matter how hard the word, did not speak without hope. We are a community with a future, for God has given us a future. We do not lose hope, ever.

What is the underlying, unshakable basis for our hope?

How can a warning lead to hope?

How can pain produce change and foster hope?

IF YOU WANT TO KNOW MORE

Read the oracles against other nations in Jeremiah 46–51 for additional words of warning.

Look up Nebuchadnezzar, Pharaoh Neco, and Babylon in a Bible dictionary.

Mark of Obedient Community
The faith community knows that its hope springs from its willingness to hear the word of the Lord and to trust that God will not abandon God's people.

"You who live on the earth,
   you are finally caught in your own trap!
The time has come; the day draws near.
On the hills panic, not glory.
   Look, the day! Look, it comes! . . .
Doom has arrived! The staff blossoms, and pride
   springs up!"   —Ezekiel 7:7, 10

7 The Day of the Lord Has Come

OUR HUMAN CONDITION

With tears and pain we discover our own ways judge us. We can't buy our way out. We can't blame anyone else. We are accountable.

ASSIGNMENT

Many Bible students skip over Ezekiel. The visions are bizarre, the poetry obscure, the imagery symbolic. But don't be put off. The form may be complicated, but the message is simple. The instruction of the priestly prophet is profound and clear once we get inside the oracles.

We will omit the oracles against other nations; but we will not forget that Ezekiel, like the other prophets, wants us to know God judges and rules all the nations of the world. Look for the meaning, the main point, in the detailed imagery. Watch for the recurring phrase, "You will know that I am the Lord."

CONTEXT

Who
Ezekiel

Where
Babylonian Exile, a thousand miles from Jerusalem, in the heart of the Babylonian Empire, which is modern-day Iraq.

When
597-571 BC

Condition of the People
The prophet Ezekiel is born during the reform of King Josiah and is deported to Babylon in an early exile in 597 BC with over ten thousand other Jews. In exile, the people are political prisoners, free to live, have jobs and families, and even worship as they choose. They just cannot return to their homeland.

Ezekiel prophesies during the same time period as Jeremiah. Jeremiah is speaking in Jerusalem. Ezekiel is speaking from Babylon, in exile, to the people in Jerusalem.

Main Message
God is going to allow Judah, Jerusalem, and the Temple to be destroyed and any remaining citizens of Judah exiled.

PRAYER

Pray daily before study:

"Don't leave me all alone, Lord!
   Please, my God, don't be far from me!
Come quickly and help me,
   my Lord, my salvation!" (Psalm 38:21-22).

Prayer concerns for the week:

Day 1 Ezekiel 1–3 (visions of the chariot and the scroll, sentinel for Israel) ✓

Day 2 Ezekiel 4–7 (symbols of the siege, the coming judgment) ✓

Day 3 Ezekiel 8–11 (Temple visions, judgment and promise) ✓

Day 4 Ezekiel 12–16 (symbols of Exile, false prophets and prophetesses, useless vine, unfaithful foundling, God's faithless bride) ✓

Day 5 Ezekiel 17–18; 20; 24 (the two eagles and the vine, the cedar, individual responsibility, Israel continues to rebel, God promises restoration, the boiling pot, death of Ezekiel's wife) ✓

Day 6 "The Word of the Lord" and "Marks of Obedient Community"

Day 7 Rest, pray, and attend class.

THE WORD OF THE LORD

Ezekiel, a contemporary of Jeremiah, was born during the reform of King Josiah. He and his wife, presumably in their early twenties, were carried off with King Jehoiachin and his royal entourage in the first deportation to Babylon (597 BC). Nebuchadnezzar placed Ezekiel in a settlement on the Chebar canal called "Tel-abib."

"Alongside Babylon's streams, / there we sat down, / crying because we remembered Zion" (Psalm 137:1). While Jeremiah prophesied in Jerusalem, Ezekiel prophesied and gave counsel to the exiles settled on the canal in Babylon.

God's Mobility

The "LORD's glory" swooped down upon Ezekiel during the fifth year of his exile when he was about thirty years old. As you read the vision in Ezekiel 1, remember Ezekiel is experiencing God. He is trying to describe what words fail to describe. Notice how often he says "like" or "the form of." Ezekiel does not see God but only "the glory" enthroned above a blazing chariot of fire.

Here are a few tips: The number four is all encompassing, as in all four directions, or the four corners of the earth. God goes everywhere. The amber color, the jewels, the burnished bronze, the crystal—all point to the magnificent splendor of the throne of God. Four living creatures, servants of God, dart to and fro at God's bidding. Wherever the spirit goes, they go. The four faces—human, lion, bull, and eagle (Ezekiel 1:10)—have been given different interpretations. They hint of creation, humanity, the animal and the bird kingdom. They symbolize strength and power.

The wheels of the chariot are crucially important. Wheels within wheels represent freedom and mobility. God has been confined to Jerusalem, resident in the Temple, present at the altar of sacrifice. Ezekiel now learns God can go wherever God wants to go. When the wheels moved, "they moved in any of the four directions, they moved without swerving" (1:17). God traveled to Babylon along with the exiles. They walked in fetters behind the creaking wheels of military chariots. God flew through the air in a chariot of fire. The people of God have moved; God has moved with them, not in a box like the ark of the covenant but high and lifted up, above all nations.

The rims of the wheels are full of eyes (1:18), eyes all over the place, moving with the wheels within the wheels. God can see anything; God sees everything. No use hiding or moving to another town. God sees and knows. God is with us.

When have you ever felt you moved away from God? When have you felt God's all-seeing presence? What helped you find God again?

In dramatic fashion, God asked Ezekiel to open his mouth and eat the scroll (3:1). God had written on it, front and back, lamentations and woes (2:9-10). No room for interpretations or additions. Take it straight. It contained everything he needed to say. The scroll tasted "as sweet as honey" (3:3).

God's words, spoken by the prophet, would be simple. Would the people back in Jerusalem listen? God tells Ezekiel that God doesn't know for sure whether they will repent. "Whether they listen or whether they refuse, since they are a household of rebels, they will know that a prophet has been among them" (2:5).

They are a hardheaded bunch, those people of Jerusalem, with stubborn hearts. So God gives them a prophet in Babylon as tough as they are (3:8-9). Never did a prophet appear with a harder "forehead" or a more stubborn will than the strange visionary by the Chebar. He was in a trance for seven days, but he came out speaking strong words (3:16-21). The uncompromising message was aimed at Judah, yet it still contained a hint of hope for repentance.

When have you felt like God asked you to proclaim an uncompromising message to someone with a stubborn heart?

Siege on a Brick, the Shaved Head

Not even Isaiah or Jeremiah acted out oracles as dramatically as Ezekiel. No wonder the exiles at the Chebar gathered around the prophet each evening when the day's work was done. What would he do next?

We can imagine that in Jerusalem, during the lull between the two invasions, about 593 BC, folks were saying, "The worst is over. God has come through for us once again. We are saved." And in Babylon, many exiles were whispering, "No use trying to adapt to this place. Soon we will be going home" (see Jeremiah 29:5-7).

So Ezekiel was tied up with ropes to symbolize slavery (Ezekiel 3:25; 4:8); didn't open his mouth (3:26); made a bread of tasteless grain and beans over dried cow dung (4:9, 15); measured bread and water in survival rations (4:10-11); drew a relief map of Jerusalem on a sun-dried brick and like a child at play built siegeworks against it (4:1-3); lay on his left side for 390 days as punishment for Israel, then on his right side 40 days as punishment for Judah (4:4-8).

Do you get the picture? Long siege, terrible deprivation, total destruction. Nobody is going home for a while. In fact, more exiles will soon be joining those in Babylonia.

If that picture didn't penetrate the hard foreheads and stubborn hearts, the shaved head should. What is Ezekiel doing now? Come and see. Why, he's burning one third of his hair in the fire. You can smell it. He's chopping one third of his hair with a sword, fine as parsley. He's scattering the rest of his hair in the wind. No, wait, he's grabbing part of that and throwing it into the fire, too, except for a few strands he's hiding in his robe. Only a meager remnant will even make it as exiles.

The prophet doesn't spell out the sins, only says Judah has acted just like other nations. Actually, they behaved even worse (5:7). Later Ezekiel would express fiery wrath toward puppet king Zedekiah for breaking his oath to Nebuchadnezzar, thereby bearing false witness before God by joining forces of rebellion with Egypt (17:11-16).

How do you think religious people will be judged? In what sense might we be held more accountable because we have been given greater guidance?

The Day of the Lord

For many of the prophets, doomsday was coming but was quite a way off. Now Ezekiel says the time of retribution has come. The awful "day of the Lord" foretold by Amos had arrived. "Your doom has come to you" (Ezekiel 7:7, NRSV). God will "judge you according to your ways" (7:8). Often the judgment of God seems fair, consequences for actions. Those who tell lies become known as liars and cannot be trusted. Those who commit adultery violate their marriage, and their home disintegrates. Many who steal are caught and called thieves. Those who are greedy and selfish generally live lives of isolation from other people. Not always, but often judgment comes according to our ways.

"They will hurl their silver into the street" (7:19). It doesn't do any good to throw money at most of our major life problems. It doesn't help to throw money at a rebellious child or at a disintegrating marriage. When a deadly disease or tragic accident comes, our gold and silver are impotent. We can't buy off God. When judgment comes, our "gold will seem unclean" (7:19).

When have you, your family, or your community experienced fair consequences for your actions? How did you respond to these consequences?

Flight Over the Temple

Some people wonder how Ezekiel knew the intimate details of the Temple even though he was in Babylon. Keep in mind that priestly families owned no land; they were paid by tithes and offerings and earned their keep by presiding at the prayers and sacrifices. The office was hereditary. They were descendants of Aaron, the levitical priesthood. So Ezekiel, like Jeremiah, would

NOTES

have been taken to the Temple by his father, placed in training at an early age, and allowed to serve as priest while still a young man. He knew the Temple like the back of his hand.

So when the Spirit of the Lord grabbed him by the hair of his head, lifted him up in a vision, and transported him to Jerusalem (Ezekiel 8:2-3), the prophet knew where he was. The glory of "Israel's God" was there (8:4); but, oh, the detestable practices that were being done there too (8:6). He saw creeping things displayed as idols (8:10). And the seventy elders of Israel were waving incense pots over the idols in prayer (8:11). He knew at least one of these respected leaders by name.

But wait! It is worse than that. In their heart of hearts the elders believe that God has gone from Israel, that foreign gods will save them. Worst of all, they believe God does not know what they are thinking (8:12).

They have idols in their hearts (14:3, 7). Abomination! God says, "Come back! Turn away from your idols and from all your detestable practices " (14:6). The Almighty wants a people who have a heart for God.

At the north gate women were weeping in front of Tammuz, the Babylonian god of the life-death cycle (8:14). In the inner court, men, probably priests, sat facing the east, their backs to the Temple, bowing toward the daily birth of the sun god of Egypt (8:16). Idolatry and paganism had invaded the very house of God.

A sense of individual responsibility emerges in Ezekiel as in Jeremiah. When the Lord's scribe clothed in linen put a mark on the forehead of those who sighed and groaned over the detestable practices in the Temple, he differentiated between individual innocence and guilt (9:3-6).

Note the similarity of chapter 10 to chapter 1. Yes, here is the Lord's glory, riding in the fiery chariot again—same wheels, same four directions, same cherubim, same eyes. Now the glory stopped at the east gate (10:19). What is happening in the Temple vision? The Lord's glory is leaving the Temple! Are you certain? Yes, "these were the same living creatures that I saw underneath Israel's God at the Chebar River" (10:20). God has already been to Babylon, and now God is departing the Temple for good. Why did the Lord's glory visit the east gate last? Because that's the main gate, the processional gate, the way God, the king, hundreds of priests, and thousands of worshipers entered the Temple on the great festival days. God is going out the way God came in! The people wanted the creeping things, the sun god, and Tammuz. Let those gods protect the Temple now.

Ezekiel wondered if any remnant would be left (11:13). Yes, because little settlements of Jews had been scattered among various countries. God says, "I've provided some sanctuary for them in the countries to which they've gone" (11:16). God will not abandon; God will not allow the remnant to perish. But more than that, God was doing a new thing. "I will give them a single heart, and I will put a new spirit in them . . . so that they may follow my regulations and carefully observe my case laws. They will be my people, and I will be their God" (11:19-20).

Symbol of Exile

Because the people in Jerusalem would not see or hear, Ezekiel was instructed to act out for the people already in exile the going into exile and the king's attempted escape (Ezekiel 12:1-16). The prophet put a knapsack on a stick, dug a hole through the wall, and crawled out during the night. That's the way King Zedekiah would try to leave Jerusalem. But Zedekiah would be caught, blinded, and dragged off to Babylon (12:12-13).

Individual Responsibility

For centuries Israel's teachings included the idea that the sins of parents would bring suffering upon the children to "the third and the fourth generation" (Exodus 34:7) and quoted the proverb, "When parents eat unripe grapes, the children's teeth suffer" (Ezekiel 18:2). Now a flash of spiritual insight, no doubt grounded in the early covenant laws, blazes across the religious horizon. The one who sins is the one who is responsible—parent or child (18:3-4). You don't have to be responsible for the sins of your ancestors. Neither can you blame your ancestors for your sins. Turn. Return. Break loose through the power of God.

Are we holding this mystery in balance? What does this teaching have to say to us in our day?

Ezekiel as a Sign

Ezekiel's wife died (Ezekiel 24:18). She was the delight of his eyes. In the morning she was alive; in the evening she was gone. The harsh instruction from God was that Ezekiel should not weep a tear, not permit a funeral, not allow mourners to wail the traditional laments, not eat the traditional burial meal with friends. When the elders asked why he acted so strangely, he was to say,

The LORD God proclaims: I'm about to make my sanctuary impure, the pride of your strength, the delight of your eyes. Your heart's desire, the sons and your daughters you left behind, will fall by the sword. You will do as I have done. You will neither cover your upper lip nor eat in human company. Your turbans will be on your heads, and your sandals on your feet. You won't mourn or weep. You will waste away in your guilt, all of you groaning to each other (24:21-23).

The pain will be too deep for tears when the city dies.

MARKS OF OBEDIENT COMMUNITY

A thousand voices shout at us from all sides. Some are warnings; some are wooings. Some warnings come from God's Word; some come from human fears. On one hand, listening to every warning could make us cowards, afraid to get out of bed. Pity the Christian who is so timid as to refrain from the life God gives. Yet God gives deep moral and religious warnings. Those who betray these warnings will suffer.

The faith community listens carefully to warnings but distinguishes between shouts that spring from human fears and the deep moral and religious warnings that come from God.

How can we distinguish fears that sap our courage from brave warnings that would save our souls?

Mark of Obedient Community
The faith community heeds God's moral and religious warnings. When we do not follow God's ways, we experience consequences.

IF YOU WANT TO KNOW MORE

Read the chapters we didn't have time to read, Ezekiel 19; 21–23.

"He asked me, 'Human one, can these bones live again?'
"I said, 'LORD God, only you know.'
"He said to me, 'Prophesy over these bones, and say to them, Dry bones, hear the LORD's word! The LORD God proclaims to these bones: I am about to put breath in you, and you will live again.' "
—Ezekiel 37:3–5

8 God Cleanses and Renews

OUR HUMAN CONDITION

How do we cope in exile? We didn't want to come. We don't feel at home. Sometimes we complain, sometimes repent. No sense putting down roots or making friends. We plan to go home soon.

ASSIGNMENT

Tough material! But don't let the obscure imagery, the harsh judgments, or the tedious detail of the Temple keep you from hearing Ezekiel's unique word from the Lord. Rejoice in the promise of Word and Spirit in the valley of dry bones. Relish the assurance of the river of grace flowing from the throne of the Temple.

CONTEXT

Who
Ezekiel

Where
Babylonian Exile, a thousand miles from Jerusalem, in the heart of the Babylonian Empire, which is modern-day Iraq.

When
587-571 BC

Condition of the People
The prophets have spoken. Jerusalem is razed. Able-bodied young people, professionals, skilled workers, and priests, not killed by famine, disease, or war, are marched off to Babylon. Only the very poor are left in Jerusalem. Theologically, some believed God let them down. God is absent.

In exile, the Jews are allowed to become prosperous. They are allowed to live in settlements, marry, have families, and enjoy conversation and prayer. There is no chance of rebellion. Jerusalem is destroyed and they are too far away. The Jews that are trying to be faithful are able to adapt their religious practices from sacrifices at the Temple to the study of the Torah and prayer. They talk of one day returning to Jerusalem.

Main Message
Ezekiel: One day, God will restore Jerusalem and Israel. But the people in exile must now accept punishment, acknowledge personal responsibility, and believe in the assurance that God will look after their future. God is their shepherd. God will bring them home again.

PRAYER

Pray daily before study:

"Remember your promise to me, your servant;
　it has given me hope.
Even in my suffering I was comforted
　because your promise gave me life"
　　　　(Psalm 119:49-50, GNT).

Prayer concerns for the week:

Day 1 Ezekiel 33–34 (God's justice and mercy, fall of Jerusalem, shepherds of Israel, God the true shepherd) ✓

Day 2 Ezekiel 35–36 (judgment against Edom, ✓ cleansing of Israel)

Day 3 Ezekiel 37 (valley of dry bones, Israel and Judah united) ✓

Day 4 Ezekiel 40–45 (God's glory returns, levitical ✓ priests, holy district)

Day 5 Ezekiel 47–48 (river of mercy and healing, division of the land) ✓

Day 6 "The Word of the Lord" and "Marks of Obedient Community"

Day 7 Rest, pray, and attend class.

THE WORD OF THE LORD

Let's pause and ask what really happened to the Judeans after 587 BC. We have a good amount of historical data in Babylonian records. The able-bodied, the young men and women, the artisans, the scholars, the professionals, and the priests—those who were not killed by war, famine, or disease—were marched off to Babylon. Unlike the Assyrians, the Babylonians did not replace the exiles with foreigners. Instead, they simply left behind in Judah a scattering of poor, rural people who worked the ravaged land and a handful of scavengers making do in the rubble of Jerusalem. The worst scenarios of the prophets were realized.

Babylonia

The Babylonians treated the exiles with restraint and permitted many to become prosperous across the years. The artisans worked at their specialties. The scholars and teachers joined faculties at schools and libraries. The former king of Judah, Jehoiachin, no longer capable of any kind of insurrection, dined at the table of the king (2 Kings 25:27-30).

Many exiled Jews maintained the irrigation canals and worked in the fields. They were allowed to live in settlements, to marry and have families, to enjoy freedom of conversation and prayer. Rebellion was out of the question.

Once Jerusalem was sacked, reality set in. Many Judean exiles followed the advice of Jeremiah and Ezekiel to build houses, work, and become a part of the economic community (Jeremiah 29:5-7).

The Jewish community in Babylon adapted its religious practices, its culture, even its language, leaving a legacy still felt today. Sacrifices could no longer be offered in the Temple, so Jewish traditions in the Torah were discussed. The prayers of the people substituted for the sacrifices of burnt offering. They no longer needed priests for the Temple, so teachers called rabbis emerged. These lay teachers taught the children and instructed the people in the ways of Torah. They began to reinterpret God's providential care to make sense of the Exile. They talked about returning to Jerusalem and met regularly in small groups for prayer and study. They sang the ancient hymns, composed new ones, remembered the traditions of the ancestors, discussed the Exodus deliverance, and pondered the warnings of the prophets. Jewish settlements in other parts of the Diaspora developed similar clusters for study and prayer.

Fall of Jerusalem

Talk about understatement! The prophets, for a century and a half, had been doing everything they knew to dramatize the potential havoc. Now the announcement of Jerusalem's ruin is made in a single statement. A lonely, bedraggled escapee comes to Ezekiel and says simply, "The city has fallen!" (Ezekiel 33:21). That's it—no emotion, no embellishment.

God's Word is amazing. It is silent where we would be loud, loud where we would be silent. For some time Ezekiel has been unable to speak, except for prophecies of destruction (3:26-27). Now his tongue is loosened, and a fresh word is on his lips (33:22). In this time of lament, the prophet gives words of interpretation, meaning, and hope.

When we grieve, we often deny reality, express anger, blame God and others. Healing requires accepting reality. Health demands persons take responsibility for their own actions. We need not continue living as we do. God never closes the door to turning. We can redirect our lives. When have you consciously redirected your life?   *At the trace.*

Where in your life might you need to consciously redirect your life right now?

The prophet had been faithful in sounding the warning trumpet. Had he not, he would have been derelict in his duties and would have been guilty too. But some people were claiming that God is not just (33:17, 20). The prophet insists that they accept culpability. It is their ways that are unjust; God's righteous justice is precisely what they have been up against.

Shepherds of Israel

Who were "Israel's shepherds" (Ezekiel 34:2)? The kings to be sure, for they were God-ordained to look after the people's welfare. But in Ezekiel 34, the shepherds include the leaders, the royalty, the priests connected to the Temple, and the false prophets who looked after their own interests.

God will now take over the job personally. God will gather the wounded, the abandoned, the weak. God will search for the lost. Notice that the prophet makes a distinction between the fat sheep and the lean (34:16, 20). No longer does God judge the entire society as a single entity; Ezekiel allows for personal guilt and innocence. Part of the new message from Ezekiel is individual accountability within the community.

In your faith community, how do you understand corporate accountability versus personal accountability?

God, the true shepherd, will still need a servant leader. It will be "my servant David" (34:23-24). Will God restore the dynasty of David? Or is this a vision of someone greater than David, a messianic prince who will rule over a "covenant of peace" (34:25)? The people in exile must now listen to fresh prophetic words—acceptance of punishment, acknowledgment of personal responsibility, and assurance that God will look after their future.

All who wail the songs of lament, all who weep from tragedy or chastisement, now hold fast to this promise: God will be your true shepherd, will heal your wounds and bring you home again. God's redemptive purpose can be delayed but not defeated.

Judgment Against Edom

Prophecies against Edom seem like an interruption. Amos, Obadiah, and Isaiah had spoken oracles against these desert kinfolk. We know that Edom helped Babylonian soldiers round up Jews fleeing Judah. To Edom God says, "I will act according to the anger and zeal you displayed when you dealt with them so hatefully" (Ezekiel 35:11). The oracle intends to show that Israel's land will one day be restored and that even the Edomites will be pushed aside. Don't forget that the Lord judges all the nations, not just Israel.

Cleansing the Spirit of Israel

For the deportees, the theological problem was this: Evidently their God had let them down. Foreigners ridiculed them. Were the gods of Babylon stronger? Had they won? The ancients believed wars were fought between the gods—the stronger ones winning, the weaker ones losing. People were saying that it was a sad day for the God of Israel. The "eternal Temple" was in a heap. In fact, the destruction was so complete that the God of the Jews was humiliated, perhaps destroyed. Think how many people today, when tragedy strikes, wonder why God did not prevent the disaster. They often experience God as absent. They question the power of God.

When have you wondered if God had any power?

Ezekiel argued that the power of God was seen precisely in the punishment (36:16-21). God did not lose; God used Babylon, even with all its false idols, to punish a wicked people. But now, with the land covered with blood, God will show power again. God will purify the remnant people and take them back to their land (36:24-25). The purpose is not merely to save Israel; it is to glorify the power of God. "House of Israel, I'm not acting for your sake but for the sake of my holy name" (36:22).

How will God do this mighty deed? By cleansing their hearts and ushering them home. By washing Israel. Symbolic purification was prescribed for ceremonial uncleanness. Repentance and obedience were called for, of course, for the ritual is not magic. But God says, "I will sprinkle clean water on you, and you will be cleansed of all your pollution. I will cleanse you of all your idols" (36:25). The land and the people will be washed clean by the grace of God. Why will God perform this mighty work? Ezekiel says it is to show that God is God.

Describe a testimony you have heard when someone told of the amazing power God has to cleanse a heart. What was said about the power of God to forgive, to cleanse, and to restore?

Valley of Dry Bones

When despair is heaviest, God gives the strongest encouragement. God asked, "Can these bones live again?" (Ezekiel 37:3). That was the question every Jew was asking: Can this bedraggled, scattered nation, which is no longer a nation, ever live again? The answer? "Prophesy over these bones, and say to them: Dry bones, hear the LORD's word!" (37:4). Suddenly the Creation story in Genesis became the framework for restoration. Life begins with the word of God. Ezekiel must speak the word of God to a dead Israel. But just as created man and woman were not living souls until God breathed into them the spirit of life, so the dry bones began to rattle but were not yet alive.

The breath, the wind, the *rûah*, the spirit of God, would give Israel life, individually and collectively (37:9-10). "I will put my breath in you, and you will live. I will plant you on your fertile land, and you will know that I am the LORD. I have spoken, and I will do it. This is what the LORD says" (37:14). God's Holy Spirit can re-birth a person and give new life to a church. *Word* and *Spirit*, God's twofold plan for a people of God to be reborn.

The Holy Temple

Ezekiel's oracles are often bizarre but seldom boring. Abruptly, in Ezekiel 40, he begins to describe the new Temple. Keep in mind this description is a vision, not a blueprint. Ezekiel is still in Babylon (40:1). What is happening here? The oracle motivates as well as predicts. Prophets energize with visions of hope.

God becomes guide and shows Ezekiel every nook and cranny of the new Temple in Jerusalem. Ezekiel reports in meticulous detail. The date? About 570 BC, more than a dozen years after the destruction, when the Jews are depressed in spirit, totally destitute of resources. The place of the vision? Babylon—hundreds of miles and seeming light years away from Israel. The prophet, who for years proclaimed doom, dramatically changes his message to one of hope and resurrection.

But this Temple is different, taller and wider to emphasize the holiness of God. It will not be adjacent to the royal palace but will be entirely separate. The kings have sinned and have let the people down. God will rule the people again. Let the prince be separate and be a servant.

Notice the emphasis on purity of worship. The faithful priests, descendants of Zadok, will be privileged to offer the sacrifice (40:46; 44:15). The other levitical priests, who participated in Israel's apostasy, will be relegated to doing chores in the Temple (44:10-14). This new priesthood symbolizes a new beginning of holy worship. Now the priests will help the people abandon their sins. The rituals of worship will be done properly because they will come straight from new hearts. In this new era, the people's lives will reflect covenant and justice.

The River of Mercy and Healing

Did you notice? The "LORD's glory" appeared to Ezekiel by the waters of the river Chebar (Ezekiel 1:28). That same "LORD's glory," whose scribe took coals of fire from the altar and scattered them over the city, stopped at the east gate, rose up, and departed the Temple before the destruction (10:1-19; 11:22-25). Now, in the vision, the "LORD's glory" will return to God's Temple (43:1-5).

God's salvation will not be confined to the Temple but rather will pour out of it like a mighty river of healing grace (47:1-12). Instead of being deepest in the Temple, it's but a trickle there. The water of salvation comes from the throne of grace, out the south side, then east. The water is ankle-deep, then knee-deep, then waist-deep, then so deep and wide it could not be crossed (47:3-5).

It will enter the great Jordan rift—the longest rift on the earth's crust—and go to the Dead Sea—the lowest and saltiest sea on the earth's surface (Ezekiel 47:8). The water will make the Dead Sea clean; even fish will swim in its fresh waters (47:9). Israel (and we) learned a lesson: God is free to be God. God's healing compassion will once again flow from the mercy seat. It will flow to the lost, to those who live in a spiritual desert, to those who are dead like the saline waters of the Dead Sea. Healing and health shall pour from God and from God alone.

Trees will line the river with fruit for nourishment and leaves for healing (47:7, 12). They flourish all year long. The vision of the Temple now bursts into a messianic dream of wholeness and health for the whole world.

The land must be divided among the people as in the first distribution. This time, all twelve tribes will receive equal distribution. (Notice the symbolism of justice, for in actuality all the tribes are thoroughly mixed up.) No Samaria or Judah but one Hebrew people, like before. Each family will be given its inheritance. As the prophet Micah envisioned,

NOTES

"All will sit underneath their own grapevines,
    under their own fig trees.
There will be no one to terrify them;
    for the mouth of the LORD of heavenly forces
      has spoken" (Micah 4:4).

The hope for the future now reaches beyond specific measurements. Ezekiel's geography is no longer exact. In picture language the area is roughly the size of Solomon's kingdom (Ezekiel 48). Ezekiel's mind is so filled with God's Spirit that he sees God's ultimate vision. The resurrection of the covenant people will be glorious.

MARKS OF OBEDIENT COMMUNITY

We live in an uprooted society. Some of us have been located in new places; all of us have been transported into new life experiences. We cannot go home; we are exiles.
    What in our faith anchors us?

We do have a home! We are not without roots. We have a memory. We have an identity. Exiles we may be, but we have a future homeland and a planned homecoming.
    In our society we are surrounded by people who feel like exiles, cut off forever from a home. What can we do to help these exiles feel at home? feel at home in God?

IF YOU WANT TO KNOW MORE

Do some research on the Babylonian Empire. See what you can discover about Nebuchadnezzar's famous hanging gardens.
    Ezekiel 25–32 and 38–39 were not included in daily assignments. Read them if time permits.

NOTES

Mark of Obedient Community
Obedient community turns exile into remembering. We rehearse our traditions. We claim our identity. We declare the God to whom we belong.

"Those who hope in the LORD
will renew their strength;
they will fly up on wings like eagles;
they will run and not be tired;
they will walk and not be weary."
—Isaiah 40:31

9 God Will Save

OUR HUMAN CONDITION

We've lost everything. We're suffering. No one seems to care. What is there to wait for? How can we trust that our circumstances will change?

ASSIGNMENT

Read Isaiah 40:28-31 aloud each day until you know it by heart.

The first word in Isaiah 40–55 is "comfort," for these messages come after the destruction of Jerusalem. Sometimes called "Isaiah of the Exile," these Scriptures have inspired great music and art and have given comfort to millions of people. They include the great servant passages. Read like a thirsty person searching for water or like a watcher scanning the sky for the first light of dawn.

CONTEXT

Who

Isaiah of the Exile: Isaiah, the prophet from Jerusalem, which we studied in Session 4, warned the people before the Fall of Jerusalem in chapters 1–39. These chapters are often referred to as First Isaiah. Prophets either added to his writings or wrote the latter chapters of Isaiah in his name. This session's readings, chapters 40–55, are attributed to Isaiah of the Exile, sometimes referred to as Second Isaiah.

Where

In Exile

When

During the Babylonian Exile (between 587 and 515 BC)

Condition of the People

Although the people are able to work, marry, worship, and even prosper, they are living under foreign rule. Spiritually, they have lost hope. They feel God has left them.

Main Message

Judgment, shocking and devastating, has been accomplished; God is now ready to save. God will set the people free. Exiles are to wait, trust, and be ready.

PRAYER

Pray daily before study:

"But me? I will hope. Always.
    I will add to all your praise.
My mouth will repeat your righteous acts
    and your saving deeds all day long.
    I don't even know how many of those there are!
I will dwell on your mighty acts, my Lord.
    LORD, I will help others remember nothing but
        your righteous deeds" (Psalm 71:14-16).

Prayer concerns for the week:

Day 1 Isaiah 40–42 (comfort, trial of the nations, servant of the Lord)

Day 2 Isaiah 43–45 (restoration and blessing, absurdity of idol worship, the Lord's anointed)

Day 3 Isaiah 46–48 (humiliation of Babylon, redemption)

Day 4 Isaiah 49:1–52:12 (the servant's mission, Zion restored, the servant's humiliation, deliverance)

Day 5 Isaiah 52:13–55:13 (the suffering servant, assurance, eternal covenant of peace)

Day 6 "The Word of the Lord" and "Marks of Obedient Community"

Day 7 Rest, pray, and attend class.

DISCIPLE FAST TRACK

THE WORD OF THE LORD

The historical context of the great Book of Isaiah covers nearly two centuries. Some scholars argue for one prophet with editing and later additions; others suggest a school of Isaiah prophets who revered their teacher. But all agree to the unusual spiritual power of this monumental book. Like a mountain range with towering peaks, this magnificent book includes the writings of perhaps three prophets: Isaiah son of Amoz, or "Isaiah of Jerusalem" (Isaiah 1–39); Second Isaiah, also called "Isaiah of the Exile" or "Isaiah of Babylon" (40–55); and Third Isaiah, or "Isaiah after the Exile" (56–66). We have separated the three parts of Isaiah to keep our sense of history clear. Judaism kept them together to give, in one great book, the full sweep of the Exile experience.

As we open Isaiah 40, promises of hope replace the warnings of doom we read in Isaiah 1–39.

> "Comfort, comfort my people,
>   says your God" (40:1).

Judgment, shocking and devastating, has been accomplished; God is now ready to save. Isaiah of the Exile sees the discouraged faces of his fellow exiles, but his heart is filled with joy. The people don't know it, but God is going to set them free. In language reminiscent of previous prophets, especially Isaiah of Jerusalem, he presents the great affirmations about God in a fresh way.

Isaiah's Call

We join Isaiah, sitting in the great council hall of heaven. Voices are speaking from the throne of God. Isaiah of the Exile, like all the prophets, receives a call. His call is simple: "Call out!" With the normal prophetic hesitancy, Isaiah cautiously asks, "What should I call out?" (Isaiah 40:6). He heard the exact message he was to declare:

> "The grass dries up; the flower withers,
>   but our God's word will exist forever" (40:8).

All else is transitory. God's word will accomplish God's purpose, for God's word and God's purpose are one.

Mighty Babylon, with all her pomp and power, is like the grass of the desert. When the hot wind, the breath of God's Spirit, blows over it, it will wither and die. The word of God will govern.

In Isaiah 40:9, Zion is the bearer of the good news to Judah that God is returning with the exiles: Tell the towns of Judah (that is, the people who used to live in Judah) that God is coming. They have suffered long enough; they have been punished more than necessary.

Now Isaiah's voice is like the voice of God. "Comfort, comfort" (40:1). Why? Because God's way will go right through the desert.

It will not go in roundabout ways. It will go straight as the crow flies. It will be smooth, without precipitous heights or dangerous valleys (40:3-4). It will be free of enemies. Even in the great stretches of desert God will feed and water the people like a shepherd who knows the way and cares for his flock (40:11).

> "The poor and needy seek water, and there is none,
>   their tongues are parched with thirst,
> I the LORD will respond to them. . . .
> I will make the desert into ponds
>   and dry land into cascades of water" (41:17-18).

God will travel the highway with them; in fact, God will lead the way just as the fire and cloud led Moses through the wilderness. Isaiah announces a new Exodus! The "LORD's glory" will walk the highway to freedom with the exiles, and everybody in the world will see it (40:5).

God Will Do a New Thing

What are the exiles to do? Wait. Trust and be ready. The God who names each star in the sky and who lifts up and brings down vast empires, who determines the course of history, is ready to do a new thing (Isaiah 41:4; 42:5-9). God has already called Cyrus of Persia to march so fast his feet will scarcely touch the ground. Though the exiles feared God had forgotten them or did not have enough power to save them, Isaiah of the Exile assures them God is strong enough to give them a new beginning (43:1-21).

Biblical faith brought into the world a new concept, the idea of *hesed*, a Hebrew word that means "constant covenant love." The covenant love of God shows constant compassion and righteousness. God would use the people of faith to teach the nations of the world how to live in just and compassionate community.

> "I . . . give you as a covenant to the people,
>   as a light to the nations" (42:6).

God never cancels the plan; *hesed* is forever. The message of Isaiah now sings with assurance and hope:

> "The things announced in the past—
>   look—they've already happened,
>   but I'm declaring new things.
>   Before they even appear,
>   I tell you about them" (42:9).

Life is not fate or happenstance. Life is certainly not influenced by figurines in the house or by the stars in the sky (47:13). If you will wait, if you will trust, God has a plan for you and will soon bring it to pass (46:10-13).

NOTES

The Almighty is coming to save you. Are you tired? Are you discouraged? Have you lost heart? Don't be afraid, for

> "those who hope in the LORD
> will renew their strength,
> they will fly up on wings like eagles,
> they will run and not be tired,
> they will walk and not be weary" (40:31).

Recall a time you have grown weary and tired of waiting on and trusting God.

How do these verses in Isaiah encourage you?

The exiles, with images of the rubble of Jerusalem in their minds, don't believe it. The words of hope bounce off their ears the same way the prophecies of doom had years before. It is understandable. Babylon seems firmly in control. Judah is no more. God seems indifferent and far away. In fact, the people murmur the same way the Hebrews murmured in the wilderness. God is oblivious to our troubles, they thought. God doesn't know and worse, doesn't care (40:27). But God "doesn't grow tired or weary" (40:28).

Have you noticed a double layer of spiritual instruction? On one hand, Isaiah speaks specifically about Babylon, Cyrus, and the return to Jerusalem. On the other hand, every reader, regardless of time or place, receives hope and encouragement. Easily we identify our own bondage. Quickly we spot our own fears. How hard it is for us to trust that God will lead us on safe ways through life's desert. How difficult for us to see a distant Cyrus hurrying to help us. How desperately we need God's encouragement to sing praise when we are still in trouble.

> "Sing a new song to the LORD;
>   sing his praise, all the world! . . .
> Sing, distant lands and all who live there! . . .
>   shout for joy from the tops of the mountains!"
> (42:10-11, GNT).

NOTES

The songs of praise announce the victory before it comes.
Have you ever considered singing songs of praise announcing the victory before it comes? Specifically, how could you practice this?

A Powerful Communicator

Few messengers have been able to convey the message of God so forcefully as Isaiah. In the courtroom scene in Isaiah 41:1-4, 21-29, God is merciless and relentless against the false gods: Who is breaking the Babylonian yoke? Not the false gods. Who has done it? "I, the LORD." God brings all the puny gods into the docket, demanding they tell about their exploits. Remember Tiglath-pileser III (Pul) and his fierce Assyrian gods? Where are they now? What about Nebuchadnezzar and the gods of Babylon? Speak up so "then we'll know that you are gods" (41:23). Silence. Other prophets laughed at the weakness of foreign gods; Isaiah goes further: They are totally powerless.

> "Look, all of them are frauds;
> their deeds amount to nothing;
> their images are a total delusion" (41:29).

When Israel stands before the court, we hear a tone more gentle than in previous prophetic trials. Earlier prophets pronounced Israel guilty and sentenced him to punishment. Isaiah softens the verdict. In 42:18-25, Israel is charged with being blind and deaf to the ways of God. He didn't understand his sins when they were pointed out to him. He thought he was being misused by God when in fact he was being punished. Now he cannot hear or see the salvation God has in store for him. Isaiah becomes one with the exiles and says,

> "We never knew what was happening;
> we learned nothing at all from it" (42:25, GNT).

Describe an experience when you actually listened and learned from the action of God.

Oracles of Salvation

We are familiar with past oracles or visions of destruction. Now Isaiah uses oracles of salvation. God proclaims the freeing word:

> "Don't fear, because I am with you,
> don't be afraid, for I am your God.
> I will strengthen you,
> I will surely help you;
> I will hold you with my righteous strong hand"
>
> (Isaiah 41:10).

God announced ahead of time he was going to do a great thing. Now in a long poem (44:24–45:13), Isaiah declares specifically that King Cyrus will be God's instrument. God calls Cyrus "his anointed" (45:1-3). Babylonian magicians and astrologers who say Babylon will rule forever are wrong. Cyrus will be shepherd king for a while because God says so (44:28).

What do we know from secular history? From Babylonian and Persian records we discover that Babylon grew weaker after mighty King Nebuchadnezzar. In 553 BC, King Nabonidus simply left Babylon and lived in the Arabian desert for ten years. His son Belshazzar (Daniel 5:1-2) ruled as co-regent during his absence.

Meanwhile, a man of remarkable ability named Cyrus rose to power. His father was a Persian king, his mother a Median princess. His grandfather was King Astyages of Media. In 550 BC, Cyrus overthrew his grandfather and moved his forces through present-day Turkey to the Aegean Sea. His contact with the Greek city states Athens and Sparta led to two centuries of conflict between Persia and Greece.

Even before Cyrus turned his forces toward Babylon, his reputation as a fair and generous man preceded him. History records that he rode into Babylon without unsheathing his sword. The gates were thrown open, and not a drop of blood was shed. His edict of 539 BC allowed Jewish exiles who wanted to return to Judah to go (Ezra 1:1-3). So the Jews would know God's hand was in it, Isaiah announced it well ahead of time.

Bel (Isaiah 46:1) is short for Bel-Marduk, god of war and well-being for Babylon. Nebo (Nabu) is his son. Isaiah says the gods will be loaded on donkeys like stacks of firewood (46:1-2). God is still in the saving business. God carried Israel from birth and will not abandon him. Israel, stubborn as he is, will be saved for the sake of God's own name (48:9).

> "I am the Lord your God
>   who teaches you for your own good,
>   who leads you in the way you should go" (48:17).

If you had kept my commandments, you wouldn't have to go through all this. Now, says God, I have to split the rock, just as I did for Moses (Exodus 17:6), so the water will gush out and my people can make it through the wilderness (Isaiah 48:21).

NOTES

Servant Songs

A new form and a new message emerge. A compassionate servant will serve as an instrument of God in the saving task. This person is not King Cyrus, who will serve as a political and military agent for freedom. Rather, the servant in four different "servant songs" brings spiritual healing. In the first song (Isaiah 42:1-4), a chosen servant is commissioned to implement justice. The other three songs are 49:1-6; 50:4-9, and the great suffering servant passage in 52:13–53:12.

Across the years, scholars have argued, and people have wondered, about the identity of the servant in these four passages. Sometimes the servant is understood as the nation Israel, sometimes as a righteous remnant within Israel, sometimes as a single righteous individual, and sometimes as a composite figure—both a group and an individual.

Whatever the identity of the servant, the servant image certainly carries within it the concept of Israel's role in God's purpose. Traditionally Jews have understood Israel to be the suffering servant, sensing the agony not only of the Exile but also of the persecution Jews have experienced across the centuries.

Isaiah sensed that redemption comes when the innocent suffer on behalf of others. Running as a quiet undercurrent through this section of Isaiah is the feeling that God suffers great anguish over the evil in the world. Christians immediately see the passion of Christ portrayed in this prophecy.

> "He was pierced because of our rebellions
>   and crushed because of our crimes.
>   He bore the punishment that made us whole;
>   by his wounds we are healed" (53:5).

For Christians the crucifixion of Jesus Christ is prophetically defined more than five centuries before Calvary. Within the Christian community is the assurance that Christ's wounds bring healing, forgiveness, and peace with God.

Whether Isaiah specifically foresaw the Savior we do not know; but we do know that he understood the eternal truth that God suffers for God's people, that innocent suffering brings vicarious healing to others, and that one day there will be righteousness and justice.

Grace and Peace

Those who say the Old Testament pictures only a God of wrath cannot have read Isaiah 54–55. Listen to the shout of victory and salvation; listen to the declaration of covenant faithfulness:

> "The mountains may shift.
> and the hills may be shaken,
> but my faithful love won't shift from you,
> and my covenant of peace won't be shaken,
> says the LORD, who pities you" (54:10).

Isaiah sounds a note of salvation for everyone. The water of mercy, the milk and wine of grace are available to all—and without price (55:1). The tragedy is that so many of us spend our money "for what isn't food" (55:2). Where do you see yourself in these words?

How would you describe the experience of laboring for that which does not satisfy?

The prophet concludes with a picture of the new and joyful Exodus:

"You will go out with celebration,
    and you will be brought back in peace.
Even the mountains and the hills will burst into song
    before you;
all the trees of the field will clap their hands" (55:12).

MARKS OF OBEDIENT COMMUNITY

The faith community acknowledges pain, hurt, even punishment, but allows itself to be comforted. We listen for God's messengers to bring us succor and signs of hope. We keep our eyes open, trusting, waiting for God's new possibilities.

When have you been part of a faith community that needed comfort?

Mark of Obedient Community
The obeying community finds comfort in knowing God is never without new possibilities and trusts even while waiting for those possibilities.

"Those who hope in the LORD will renew their strength" (Isaiah 40:31). What does that promise mean to you?

IF YOU WANT TO KNOW MORE

Look up Cyrus II of Persia and three fairly unfamiliar kings who have interesting connections: Nabonidus, Belshazzar, and Astyages.

NOTES

"The immigrants who have joined me,
    serving me and loving my name, becoming my servants,
    everyone who keeps the Sabbath without making it impure,
    and those who hold fast to my covenant:
I will bring them to my holy mountain,
    and bring them joy in my house of prayer."   —Isaiah 56:6-7

10 God's Vision for a New World

OUR HUMAN CONDITION

When reality falls short of our expectation and our dreams are shattered by disappointment, we lose our balance and fall victim to despair.

ASSIGNMENT

Compare other translations as you read these visions of end times. You may also want to compare these visions with those of earlier prophets. Note the universality of the vision, the inclusion of the foreigner and the eunuch at the holy mountain.

CONTEXT

Who
Isaiah After the Exile (Third Isaiah)

Where
Jerusalem

When
The prophet we call Third Isaiah lived in Jerusalem and spoke sometime between the beginning of the rebuilding of the Temple in 538 BC and well before 445 BC when the wall around Jerusalem was rebuilt.

Condition of the People
It has been at least fifty years since the final exile from Jerusalem. Most people returning are children of the original exiles and are going to a war-ravaged land they have never seen. Landmarks they have heard about are absent, strangers are present, and the social and religious structures are gone. Freedom and restoration has come but so have friction, injustice, and hardship.

Main Message
Isaiah is speaking to the exiles who have returned and have undertaken the difficult work of rebuilding the Temple. He proclaims that the Temple must be a house of prayer and that they are to be holy. These difficult days will pass and Israel will persevere. During this time they are to be confident in their faith and obedient in holiness. He lists problems, provides guidance for holy living, and pulls us into dreams of eternity.

PRAYER

Pray daily before study:

"God, your way is holiness!
    Who is as great a god as you, God?
You are the God who works wonders;
    you have demonstrated your strength among
        all peoples" (Psalm 77:13-14).

Prayer concerns for the week:

Day 1 Isaiah 56–57 (covenant extended to the obedient, Israel's futile idolatry) ✓

Day 2 Isaiah 58–59 (true fasting, kindness and justice, the people's transgressions, need for repentance) ✓

Day 3 Isaiah 60–61 (restoration of Jerusalem, mission to Zion, an everlasting covenant) ✓

Day 4 Isaiah 62–64 (salvation of Zion, God's mercy for the penitent) ✓

Day 5 Isaiah 65–66 (God's righteous judgment, future hope, reign of God) ✓

Day 6 "The Word of the Lord" and "Marks of Obedient Community"

Day 7 Rest, pray, and attend class.

DISCIPLE FAST TRACK

THE WORD OF THE LORD

At the beginning of Isaiah 56, the mood has changed. Many of the Israelites have walked the highway of the Lord back to Jerusalem. Not all the exiles returned, of course. Like Jews of the Diaspora everywhere, some had put down roots, gained property, raised children, and learned the ways of the people among whom they lived. Under the tolerant Persians, some, like Nehemiah, even helped in the king's court.

Those Jews who were fueled by the visions of Ezekiel's Temple or Isaiah's highway through the desert walked to Judah with their possessions on their backs or in a pushcart but with light steps and happy hearts. They came from Babylon, where many had been forced to live since the destruction of Jerusalem. The Persian victory over Babylon in 539 BC established Persian control across the two thousand miles from India to Greece, the largest Mediterranean empire to date. With the edict of Cyrus (538 BC), children and grandchildren of the exiles made their way home.

But ask yourself, What would it be like to return to a war-ravaged land after fifty or more years? And for many, to a city of rubble where you had never lived? These people are free at last, thank God, but free in a tough land where landmarks have been removed, where strangers live, where the social and religious structure has totally collapsed. The people who had been left behind had set up their own organization and had occupied the property that was abandoned. So friction was inevitable. Isaiah's prophecies of freedom and restoration came true; but the streets were not lined with trees, and justice and peace did not govern the land (Isaiah 55:12).

Isaiah 55–66 was written in Jerusalem during the postexilic period, probably after the rebuilding of the Temple but well before the rebuilding of the walls by Nehemiah. We need to read this Scripture on at least three distinct levels:

• Listen to the messenger deal with the *specific problems* of his immediate time and place. As we listen to pronouncements that were conditioned by the experiences of the returned exiles, we can learn lessons to apply to our lives.

• The messenger gives deep *spiritual insight*. His oracles give profound godly guidance for faithful living to people of all generations.

• The God-inspired dreams pull us into eternity. The oracles sometimes start out local and concrete, then expand into *end-time visions* of peace and justice for all humankind.

The new religious community must keep the old faith—right living and Sabbath observance (56:1-2). They need to rebuild on the old foundations, spiritual as well as physical (58:12). But the doors of faith need to be flung open to others as well. The prophet widens Israel's arms of inclusiveness.

"A foreigner who has joined the LORD's people should not say, 'The LORD will not let me worship with his people.'

"A man who has been castrated should never think that because he cannot have children, he can never be part of God's people" (56:3, GNT).

This teaching contrasts with an earlier law that barred such people from the assembly of the Lord (Deuteronomy 23:1). Foreigners as well as Jews who love the Lord will be welcomed in worship on the holy mountain (Isaiah 56:6-7).

The faithful were expecting a spiritual utopia with cleansed, dedicated leaders. Instead, both civic and religious leaders sadly neglected their duties. Like watchdogs that wouldn't bark, they failed to warn people of the dangers of wickedness. They were lazy, greedy, and self-indulgent. They drank too much wine and yearned for more. If such leadership continues, shouted the prophet, other peoples will come like wild animals to devour them (56:9-12).

No one since Amos had chastised people so ferociously for their sexual immorality and idolatry as this prophet. Pagan worship with high places, fertility rites, and child sacrifice was not a thing of the past. The prophet condemned those who fornicated on the hillsides where the old Canaanite cults of prostitution had been. New freedoms broke down old prohibitions. Rebellion against God persisted. People dedicated themselves to fancy clothes, expensive perfumes, and continual sexual escapades until they nearly wore themselves out (57:3-10).

God says they do not fear, do not even "remember me / or give me a thought" (57:11). Healing is offered, mercy extended to the sorrowful (57:18-19). But to those who continue in their idolatry and wickedness? The spiritual leaders have been silent; so the prophet simply explains the Lord's judgment by saying, "I will denounce your conduct" (57:12, NEB), and then adds,

"The wicked are like the churning sea that can't keep
    still.
  They churn up from its waters muck and mud.
  There is no peace, says my God, for the wicked"
                                        (Isaiah 57:20-21).

A Holy Fast

Many of the homecomers tried to be religious. They did not use their foreign statuettes or idolatrous figurines. They were more careful about Sabbath prayers. Some serious Jews prayed in public, put on rough sackcloth, and fasted. But in fierce prophetic tradition, Isaiah insists that religious exercises designed to impress God are worthless. What kind of a fast would please God? You guessed it: Remove injustice and oppression, save food to share with the hungry, take the homeless into your house, or at least help them find a place to sleep, provide clothing for the destitute, and look after your kinfolk. Oh, yes, be sure to keep Sabbath in your hearts and in your actions (Isaiah 58:6-7, 13-14). Someday everyone will recognize Sabbath as a healthful practice and make regular Sabbath pilgrimages to the Lord (66:23).

Care for one's relatives received continual emphasis so that it became a distinguishable Jewish trait. Grounded in the culture of the ancient Near East, such caring was fortified with the fifth commandment: "Honor your father and your mother so that your life will be long on the fertile land that the LORD your God is giving you" (Exodus 20:12). It was further strengthened by the commandment "Do not commit adultery" (20:14) and by intense stress on teaching moral values and religious tradition to one's children (Deuteronomy 6:6-7, 20-25). It became a proverb in Israel:

"Listen to your father, who gave you life;
don't despise your elderly mother" (Proverbs 23:22).

Within the Christian community, this Jewish truth is so fundamental that it is scandalous to think otherwise. "If someone doesn't provide for their own family, and especially for a member of their household, they have denied the faith. They are worse than those who have no faith" (1 Timothy 5:8). How are you doing in this area of your life?

What is the reward for a godly fast? God will lift your gloom. The Lord will guide your thoughts and decisions. You will be healthy and feel like a well-watered garden (Isaiah 58:10-11). But wait, something more important: You will be part of the rebuilding of the city. You will build on the old foundations of justice. You will be known as a builder, one of the righteous persons who keep a city alive.

"They will rebuild ancient ruins on your account;
the foundations of generations past you will restore.
You will be called
Mender of Broken Walls,
Restorer of Livable Streets" (58:12).

As you think about the injustice within the cities of our world, what are some ways you could be a "Restorer of Livable Streets"?

Like Isaiah of Jerusalem nearly two centuries before, the prophet pleads for people to refrain from sin, to repent, to live holy lives. But the influence of Jeremiah and Ezekiel causes him to be more personal, more individual. Notice: God will forgive and save "all of you that turn from your sins" (59:20, GNT). The community, tight as it is, is seen no longer only as a single entity.

God distinguishes between the behavior of individuals and judges accordingly.

The sins are as public as today's newscast—lying, violence, murder. People hurt people and then lie in court. Innocent people are destroyed; no one is safe (59:3-8). A heartbroken litany of lament follows a list of sins. It shows the way back into mercy and godly living (59:9-15).

But in the face of such sin, God will act.

> "[He put] on righteousness as armor
> and a helmet of salvation on his head,
> putting on garments of vengeance,
> and wrapping himself in a cloak of zeal" (Isaiah 59:17).

A Bright Future

Discouragement clouded the lives of the returned exiles. So much work to be done, such limited resources. Against this grim background, the prophet projects a vision of divine help. "The LORD's glory" will bring light to their gloom and material resources as well (Isaiah 60:1-3). Other exiles will come to help them, some by ship (60:4-5). And they did. Traders will pass through with goods from far-off lands (60:6). They did, for under Persian peace the fertile crescent was alive again. Money will come from unexpected sources. Cyrus, and later King Darius, had actually sent aid to rebuild the Temple. God will bring in foreigners to help repair the city (60:10). The message was clear. The picture was not so bleak as they thought; God would bring resources to their aid if they would work hard and keep the faith.

But wait a minute. The vision is too good to be true. God's glory will be so bright, so glorious, that Jerusalem will need neither sun nor moon (60:19-20). Violence will come to an end. Rulers will be just. Everyone will do exactly the right thing. God will name a new overseer for the city of Zion whose name will be *Peace* (60:17). God will appoint a new chief administrator whose title will be *Righteousness*. *Salvation* will be the strong walls, and *Praise* will be the gates (60:17-18). Everyone will be wearing new clothes, beautiful as a bride ready for her wedding; however, the gorgeous gown will not be made of cloth but of the saving love and righteousness of God (61:10).

It has happened again: The prophet got close to God. God elevated hope to a higher level, transformed a good future into a heavenly vision. Once again the prophet sees the far horizon.

Go to Work!

When Jesus stood up in his hometown synagogue, the elders handed him the Isaiah scroll. Jesus chose a servant passage and took on his shoulders the mission of Israel:

> "The LORD God's spirit is upon me,
> because the LORD has anointed me" (Isaiah 61:1).

DISCIPLE FAST TRACK

Israel was called to be a nation of priests, a holy people driven to teach God's word of salvation to all the world. And in their doing it, God will continually bless and strengthen.

Don't be discouraged. You are defeated now, "Abandoned," living in a place named "Deserted." I will give you and your place a new name, Beulah Land (KJV), which means "Married to the Lord." "Deserted" will become "Delight" (62:4). Trust God, and don't lose hope. Good prophets will stand at the sentinel posts. They will bark warnings. They will not be the false prophets of old who cried, "All is well, all is well," and "Peace," when there was no peace (Jeremiah 6:14; 8:11; Ezekiel 13:10).

Now, go to work! Pick up the rubble. Clear the old stones. Prepare the highway so worshipers may come. Construct the gates, the walls. You are no longer a city forsaken. You are God's city. Build! Build! (Isaiah 62:10).

Why are God's robes stained with red? Because God has been busy stomping God's opponents in the wine press of judgment.

> "I trampled down nations in my anger
>   and made them drunk on my wrath" (63:6).

Thoughts of judgment overwhelm the prophet. He intercedes on behalf of the people. O God, please come down now (64:1). Don't delay. You are the Holy One. We have sinned. "We are the clay, / and you are our potter" (64:8). Save us.

New Heavens and New Earth

God is about to create a new heaven and a new earth (Isaiah 65:17). There is no room in the new creation for a rebellious people who follow their own devices. The new era calls for a new people, people who rejoice in God. Again a vision of the new earth, of a world transformed: No babies will die; people will live to be a hundred; no one will weep. Those who build their houses will live in them. Those who plant vineyards will not have the fruit stolen from them; they will be able to enjoy the fruit of their labors (65:19-23). All nature will be in harmony. Compare 65:25, the wolf and the lamb, the lion and the ox, to the vision in 11:6-9. All nature has been disturbed by sin; therefore all nature will be healed by grace. Once again God's final purpose fills the prophet's mind with vision.

Don't be impatient. "Can a land come to birth in one day?" (66:8). God has opened the womb and will deliver (66:9).

> "As a mother comforts her child,
>   so I will comfort you. . . .
> When you see this, your heart will rejoice" (66:13-14).

The prophet brings his message to a climax by underlining the essential truths: God will usher in the new heavens and the new earth, and everyone—people from all nations, "all humanity"—will come to worship before the Lord (66:22-23).

NOTES

92

How do Isaiah's God-inspired dreams and visions give you hope?

MARKS OF OBEDIENT COMMUNITY

Like the prophet, the community of faith looks to the far horizon, holds on to a guiding vision.

Can you envision a new future, a godly future for yourself, your group, your church, your community? What would be required? Prayer? reconciliation? hard work?

If your dreams are in tune with God's dreams, how can God help you? What resources do you have? What resources do you need?

We believe God is at work, breaking down the walls of hostility, wiping away the tears of sorrow, and ushering in peace. We believe one day God will create a new heaven and a new earth where justice, goodwill, and joy will prevail. We live in that expectancy and strive toward it.

How does this vision affect your daily life?

How does it influence your faith community?

How can you work for it while you wait?

When the heart harbors hope, the human spirit can achieve great things. When did you believe in God so much, believe in yourself and in your future so much that you worked tirelessly to achieve something good?

IF YOU WANT TO KNOW MORE

Read Revelation 21:1-4, 22-26, and 22:5 and ponder the similar imagery of the kingdom of God's righteousness and peace.

Mark of Obedient Community
The obedient community, fueled by vision and sustained by hope, keeps the long view in mind but is faithful in the present.

"Is it time for you to dwell in your own paneled houses
while this house lies in ruins?
So now, this is what the LORD of heavenly forces says:
Take your ways to heart. . . .
Go up to the highlands and bring back wood.
Rebuild the temple so that I may enjoy it
and that I may be honored, says the LORD."
—Haggai 1:4-5, 8

11 God's City of Peace

OUR HUMAN CONDITION

Faced with competing priorities, we tend to focus on ourselves: Times are not good. We have our own responsibilities. This is not the time to do for others. But the right word from the right leader might get our cooperation.

ASSIGNMENT

The Ezra material gives helpful historical background for Haggai and Zechariah. Don't get bogged down in the imagery in the visions of Zechariah. You may find the Good News Translation helpful. Watch for hints that both Haggai and Zechariah look toward the coming messianic age.

CONTEXT

Who
Haggai and Zechariah

Where
Jerusalem

When
Haggai and Zechariah (520-515 BC)

Condition of the People
Jerusalem is part of the Persian Empire. Farming and herding is hard work. When the exiles first return to Jerusalem in 538 BC under the Persian king Cyrus, they start rebuilding the Temple. But after two years a new Persian emperor takes over and stops the progress because he fears rebellion. For eighteen years the Jews build their homes and businesses, but don't appeal the decision about rebuilding the Temple, even when another new emperor, King Darius, arrives. Then in 520 BC there is a drought, crops fail. The prophets Haggai and Zechariah arrive on the scene.

Main Message
Haggai: Prosperity is absent from Judah because the Temple has not been rebuilt and wealth beyond measure will follow if the Temple is rebuilt.

Zechariah: In the first eight chapters of the book, Zechariah proclaims that God is in control and promises that God will help the people finish the Temple.

PRAYER

Pray daily before study:

"Pray that Jerusalem has peace:
　'Let those who love you have rest.
　Let there be peace on your walls;
　let there be rest on your fortifications.'
For the sake of my family and friends,
　I say, 'Peace be with you, Jerusalem.'
For the sake of the LORD our God's house
　I will pray for your good" (Psalm 122:6-9).

Prayer concerns for the week:

Day 1 Haggai 1; Ezra 1–3 (time to rebuild the ✓ Temple, exiles return, foundation laid)

Day 4 Zechariah 4–6 (visions of the restored ✓ community)

Day 2 Haggai 2; Ezra 4–6 (promises and blessings, ✓ opposition to rebuilding, Passover)

Day 5 Zechariah 7–8 (kindness and mercy, not ✓ fasting; God's promises to Jerusalem and Judah)

Day 3 Zechariah 1–3 (call to repentance, visions in ✓ the night)

Day 6 "The Word of the Lord" and **"Marks of Obedient Community"**

Day 7   Rest, pray, and attend class.

THE WORD OF THE LORD

Haggai and Zechariah lived under new attitudes toward governing (Ezra 6:14). The Assyrians had ruthlessly mixed and exchanged populations to weaken social fabric. The Babylonians had reduced the Temple to ruins and had taken away as exiles the brightest and the best. But the brilliant politician Cyrus put together the Medes, the Persians, and the Babylonians into a vast empire that was more tolerant of differences in its people. Cyrus, in one of his first acts after conquering Babylon, permitted exiled peoples to return to their homes, carrying with them their sacred vessels for use in worship (Ezra 6:3-5). His theory was to encourage cooperation from the subject peoples throughout the Persian Empire.

Cyrus allowed the first wave of exiles to return to Jerusalem in 538 BC (1:1-4; 6:14). Under Cyrus's orders, Sheshbazzar, a "prince of Judah" (1:8), led nearly fifty thousand people (2:64) to return to a pile of rubble. A homeless, rootless, exiled people need more than words. They need things they can touch, things that remind them of who they are. That is why they brought the holy vessels. That is why they began to rebuild the Temple. Within two years (536 BC), even while they were trying to build houses and eke out an existence, they cleared the site and laid the foundation of the Temple (3:8-11). But suddenly the work stopped; no further Temple construction took place for sixteen years.

The returnees faced huge obstacles. Residents voiced objections. Local Persian authorities believed the effort to be seditious. Old and new landowners argued over property rights. Intermarried Israelites and non-Israelites, probably including Samaritans, had counterproposals. And they ran out of money and material. Even the king called a halt to the project (4:21). However, when King Darius the Great came to power in 521 BC, he allowed more exiles to return, bridled his Persian officials, and supported the rebuilding of the Temple (6:6-12). He appointed a new political agent, Zerubbabel, grandson of the Davidic king Jehoiachin, to lead the effort (3:2, 8).

Haggai and Zechariah

Haggai and Zechariah, two minor prophets, loom large in the rebuilding of Jerusalem (Ezra 5:1-2). They stimulated the restoration of religious and political life for the returning exiles. These two cheerleader prophets challenged the returnees to organize their religious community, work together, and rebuild the Temple.

Haggai and Zechariah succeeded where others had failed. Called by some "the fathers of Judaism," these prophets did more than encourage the rebuilding of Solomon's Temple, great task though that was. They fortified the governor's political position and elevated the high priest to religious authority. They began a reshaping of theology that would continue for five centuries, until the time of Jesus Christ. And they gave spiritual courage to the Jews to move forward in reconstruction of the country.

Haggai prophesied for only four months, as far as we know, from August to December of 520 BC. He saw that the people lacked resources and they lacked resolve. Everybody said, "It's not the right time." Times *were* tough, of course—little rain, poor crops; money ran right through their pockets.

Can't you see why this has happened? Haggai asked. God is not blessing us because you are living in paneled houses while God's house (the Temple) lies in ruins (Haggai 1:4). No wonder things are going badly.

Like earlier prophets, Haggai stirred up things with a powerful speech. Zerubbabel, governor of a disorganized city, listened. Joshua, high priest without a Temple, listened. Haggai gave a rousing proclamation on the twenty-ninth of August, 520 BC. By the middle of September the people were hard at work. The right leader at the right time who hears the whispers of God can excite a whole people to action.

Memory Becomes Vision

"Who among you is left who saw this house in its former glory?" asked Haggai (Haggai 2:3). Few raised their hands. Maybe a handful of elderly. Probably not Haggai. Certainly not Zerubbabel, grandson of Jehoiachin. But the prophet held up the memory of Solomon's Temple as a vision to inspire the people. Men and women, young and old, will have to put their shoulders to the wheel to make things happen. But if they can visualize it, they can build it. "Take courage . . . take courage . . . take courage," he shouted (2:4-5, NRSV). God is with us; don't be afraid.

What assurances did Haggai give? First, if God could bring them out of Egypt (out of Babylon too), God would help them build a Temple (2:5). Moreover, God is going to shake the whole world for more resources. God is never short of gold and silver (2:7-8).

The problem is always one of distribution. God needed to shake some pockets. Sure enough, other refugees returned, some with gold in their pockets and a love for the Temple in their hearts. King Darius sent money. Gifts of lumber and stone plus offers of labor came from unexpected sources. The Temple was completed in 515 BC, requiring about five years for construction. Haggai put great hopes in Governor Zerubbabel. In his final prophecy Haggai called Zerubbabel God's servant, and again, an expression Jeremiah used, God's "signet ring" (2:23; see Jeremiah 22:24).

Describe a time when you were involved in a church or community project and strangers and outsiders offered unexpected help.

Visions in the Night

Zechariah heard the call from God a couple of months after Haggai heard his. His visions came in the night—wild, bewildering oracles full of strange prophetic imagery. The four different-colored horses, for example, simply represent messengers going to the four corners of the earth, on patrol, to scout for God (Zechariah 1:7-17). With two thousand miles of Mediterranean territory ruled by the Persians, they report, "The whole earth is peaceful and quiet" (1:11). But God is not happy (and neither is the prophet), because Jerusalem lies in ruins while the nations are at ease (1:15). The four horns (1:18) depict the powerful nations of the world who have conquered the people of Israel and Judah and held them in exile (1:19). God will "destroy" the horns (1:21), and scattered Jews can return home.

In another night vision a man is measuring Jerusalem (2:1-2). Surveyors and engineers are at work. That's good. But some are already anxious about the immense distance and cost involved in rebuilding the walls. Don't worry about that now, says the prophet. God will protect the city, as "a wall of fire all around it" and a presence within it (2:5). Meanwhile, those of you still remaining in Babylon, come on home. You are "the apple of my eye," says the Lord (2:8, NRSV).

In 3:1-2 (NRSV), the word *Satan* would be better translated "the Adversary" (as it is in the Common English Bible), for its meaning is different from that in the New Testament. The Adversary's job is to accuse, to point a finger of guilt, this time at the high priest, Joshua. Joshua, symbolizing all of Judah, is cleansed and renewed; for God says, "I will remove the guilt of that land in one day" (3:9). God is slow to punish, quick to forgive. The mournful lamentations are over; it is time to rebuild.

Dreaming God's Dream

In the vision of Zechariah 4, *seven* represents God. Seven lamps with seven wicks in each lamp show God full of light, able to see everything, everywhere (4:2, 10). Two olive trees, Zerubbabel and Joshua, stand beside the lamps (4:3). Remember, governor and high priest, the task of rebuilding the Temple will not require slave labor or military conscription as Solomon used to build his ostentatious palaces. God's Spirit will do it. "Neither by power, nor by strength, / but by my spirit, / says the Lord of heavenly forces" (4:6).

In Chapter 8, Zechariah dreams God's dream—a faithful city where the "glory" dwells. The streets will be safe again, peaceful for little children and the elderly, even late in the evening. People from all over the world will hear about the peace of Jerusalem and be drawn to it, just as they once were driven from it. "They will be my people, and I will be their God—in truth and in righteousness" (8:8). Once again the vision hints of a joyful end time of peace (*shalom*). Then back to earth: Don't be afraid to go forward with your work. "Be strong," for "I will deliver you" says the Lord (8:13).

How we need a faithful city of peace where God's glory dwells today. What could we do to improve the quality of life for the elderly?

What could we do right now so children could play safely?

MARKS OF OBEDIENT COMMUNITY

The faithful community knows our time is now. This is our time to see and hear the plan of God. We neither daydream about yesterday's opportunities nor fantasize over tomorrow's possibilities. We accept today's task God gives us as our immediate faith response. Haggai said, "Take courage." Zechariah said, "Be strong."

What do you see God calling your DISCIPLE FAST TRACK group to do right now that will take courage and commitment?

How will we follow through on this commitment?

Where is the "iron hot" for Christian work, witness, or service?

Mark of Obedient Community
The obedient faith community accepts the task God gives us for today as our immediate faith response.

IF YOU WANT TO KNOW MORE

The First Temple, built by Solomon about 960 BC, was destroyed when the Babylonians conquered Jerusalem in 587 BC.

The Second Temple, built by the returned exiles under Zerubbabel (520-515 BC), was desecrated and damaged by the Greeks in 325 BC and desecrated again by the Seleucid Antiochus IV in 167 BC.

In 20/19 BC, Herod the Great began to restore and refurbish what was left of the Second Temple and to construct a complex of buildings around it. The renovation continued after his death and was not completed until shortly before this Temple was destroyed by the Romans in AD 70. Do some research on the different Temples. Compare this Temple to Solomon's Temple. Find out how Herod's Temple, where Jesus taught, relates to this Temple.

"Look, I am sending my messenger who will clear the
path before me;
suddenly the LORD whom you are seeking will come
to his temple.
The messenger of the covenant in whom you
take delight is coming,
says the LORD of heavenly forces." —Malachi 3:1

12 God's Mission for Israel

OUR HUMAN CONDITION

We often lose hope when everything seems to
be going against us. Sometimes we even believe
we have been forgotten by God. And then, to be
asked to share God's message that will result in
forgiveness of those against us is unthinkable.
We still feel the pain from them. We don't want to
include them.

ASSIGNMENT

Take each prophet at face value, separate and
distinct. Listen to the unique message, even if it
is limited as in Obadiah or heavily eschatological
as in Zechariah. Watch Obadiah's poetic wordplay
on "rock," the high places, Mount Esau, eagles'
soaring, and their nest among the stars (3-4). Joel's
promise (Joel 2:28-32) lays the foundation for
Peter's Pentecost sermon (Acts 2:14-42). Malachi
states God's promise in the tithe. Zechariah's
images of the Prince of Peace and the Good
Shepherd are familiar to us as later descriptions of
Jesus Christ.

Jonah would once again remind the people of the
great task: to be a light or blessing to the world.

PRAYER

Pray daily before study:

"Send your light and truth—those will
guide me!
Let them bring me to your holy
mountain,
to your dwelling place.
Let me come to God's altar—
let me come to God, my joy, my delight—
then I will give you thanks with the lyre,
God, my God!" (Psalm 43:3-4).

Prayer concerns for the week:

Day 1 **Obadiah; Amos 1:11-12; Ezekiel 35** (woe to Edom, the day of the Lord)

Day 2 **Joel 1–2** (plague of locusts, call to repentance, outpouring of the Spirit)**; Joel 3** (judgment on the nations, future blessings on Judah)

Day 3 **Malachi 1–4** (corrupt priesthood, the coming messenger, the great day of the Lord)

Day 4 **Zechariah 9–14** (the coming king, Jerusalem's strength, the scattered flock, future warfare and victory)

Day 5 **Jonah 1–4** (running from God's call, Jonah's hymn of deliverance, Nineveh repents, Jonah's anger, God's compassion)

Day 6 **"The Word of the Lord" and "Marks of Obedient Community"**

Day 7 **Rest, pray, and attend class.**

THE WORD OF THE LORD

Obadiah, like a hot desert wind, blasts the people of Edom with one brief, vitriolic message.

"The LORD God proclaims concerning Edom: . . .
I will make you of little importance among the nations;
   you will be totally despised" (Obadiah 1-2).

Who were the Edomites? The Edomites are Esau's descendants (Genesis 36:1), making their home in the rocky hills southeast of the Dead Sea and on the western edge of the Arabian desert. Their fortress capital, nestled high in the hills, was Teman (Tema), which means "rock," near today's Petra (rock) in southern Jordan.

What was Edom's sin? Uncaring toward kin in time of trouble! Even though the kinship was strained across the centuries, still, they shouldn't have pounced on Judah when invaders from the north ravaged Jerusalem (Obadiah 10-12). Worse, they gloated over Judah's misfortune, joined in the looting, even captured some runaways and gave them over to the enemy (13-14). Damnable behavior for blood relatives, claimed Obadiah, deserving the wrath of God. Where did this prophet get his understanding of blood responsibility and fair play?

When have you been guilty of uncaring attitudes toward relatives in time of trouble?

The prophecy borders on being a nationalistic diatribe against one of Judah's enemies. But it is broadened by a sense of justice. What difference does it make to you in your faith to know that every nation stands under the judgment of God?

A Time to Turn

Joel had the heart of a farmer, the soul of a poet, and the spiritual sensitivities of a priest. A person who loves the soil grieves when "the grain shrivels under the shovels" (Joel 1:17-18). As the locusts devour the vegetation, he weeps:

"Land ahead of them is like Eden's garden,
   but they leave behind them a barren wasteland" (2:3).

Joel sings like a poet.

"Tear your hearts and not your clothing.
Return to the LORD, your God,

for he is merciful and compassionate,
very patient, full of faithful love" (2:13).

The vision of a man ripping his clothes in repentance drives the spiritual point home. The prophets were not as interested in outward forms as they were in inner attitudes.
What response or action is called for by the phrase "tear your hearts" (Joel 2:13)?

Notice that Joel includes female and male, old and young, slave and free in his prophecy of the day of the Lord, a remarkable early insight into the universality of the Spirit of God: "I will pour out my spirit upon everyone" (2:28-29).
Joel connected the destruction wrought by the locusts to the coming day of the Lord, and he used the plague of locusts as a call for repentance. But even then, when people saw the hand of God in all natural phenomena, they were inclined to pray for rescue rather than for forgiveness.
Do we not today, in times of sickness, tragic natural disorders, and impending death, pray for rescue? What would it mean for us today to hear Joel's cry to mend our ways in the face of natural calamity?

Even amid the swarming locusts, Joel promises a better day (2:21-24). But he goes deeper:
"I will repay you for the years that the swarming locust . . . [has] eaten" (2:25-27). People of faith have been blessed by the promise that God will bring a blessing out of tragedy.
Describe a personal experience when God has restored for you "the years the locusts have eaten."

God Will Restore
Joel lived probably during the time of the great Persian Empire (539-331 BC) when relative peace pervaded the land.
He wants the people to love God and not lose hope in the future. Joel envisions the day when God will "restore the fortunes of Judah and Jerusalem" (Joel 3:1, NRSV). He hints at preparation for war and judgment, but his emphasis is on renewed strength and vitality. Everyone will know that "the LORD is a refuge for his people" (3:16).
The locusts will be gone, the enemies vanquished. Joel faithfully promises the final victory of God in earthly terms.

What seems to be a call to holy war becomes instead a time of God's judging all the nations.

The Great Day of the Lord

The word of the Lord to Malachi demands serious and sincere worship. The Temple has been rebuilt. The priests are in place. The city has a governor under Persian authority.

Malachi wants worship to be done properly. What elements of worship do you take seriously?

The law of Moses demanded only perfect animals for sacrifice. Would people actually cheat God by giving inferior gifts—blind, sick, or lame animals? Such practices were forbidden by the Law. "Whenever someone presents a communal sacrifice of well-being to the LORD from the herd or flock—whether it is payment for a solemn promise or a spontaneous gift—it must be flawless to be acceptable; it must not have any imperfection" (Leviticus 22:17-21).

How might we be tempted to cheat when we give gifts to God today?

Even when giving is voluntary, when we don't have to donate at all, how do we find ways to give less than we pretend?

Malachi is severe on the priests, insisting that they practice integrity and that their lips guard knowledge. If they do not speak the truths of the covenant, they cause others to stumble (Malachi 2:4-9). Similarly, in what ways might those of us who teach and preach be judged more strictly than others?

Divorce is not often mentioned by the prophets, but God says through Malachi, "because [the LORD] hates divorce. . . . Guard your own life, and don't cheat" (2:16). The call to faithfulness permeates Malachi's prophecy—faithfulness to the covenant God, to the covenant community, and to the covenant of marriage. We know divorce often does harm to the couple, to children, to families, and to the church. What is being done in your congregation to strengthen marriages?

NOTES

Malachi is a part of the prophetic tradition demanding that people return to the Lord. True worship, key to that return, includes not deceiving God. "But you say, 'How have we deceived you?' " (3:8). The answer: by failing to bring the full tithe, 10 percent, into the Lord's storehouse. Seldom in Scripture does God ask to be put to the test in keeping the Law (and the tithe, like all the rest, was part of the covenant). But look at the challenge: "Please test me in this. . . . / See whether I do not open all the windows of the heavens for you / and empty out a blessing until there is enough" (3:10).

When have you put God to this test on tithing? What were the results?

Zechariah 9–14

Zechariah 9–14, probably written by disciples of Zechariah, is composed of oracles, remembrances, and visions to fortify or balance Zechariah 1–8. We understand these passages best if we think symbolically.

Zechariah 1–8 speaks of God's victory in concrete terms—the return of Israel to Jerusalem, the victory of God in praise on Mount Zion. But that didn't happen. People were becoming discouraged; they did not see signs of God's ultimate kingdom. So Zechariah begins to see "end times." God is the Great Warrior who will redeem Israel (9:13-14). Enemies of God will be destroyed (9:1-6). Some Gentiles who love the Lord will be saved (9:7). God, who has fought against Israel because of its sins, now turns to fight for Israel (9:16). God will powerfully win the final victory. This oracle makes Israel "prisoners of hope" (9:12).

The Messiah King

In this bewildering maze of prophecy stands a glorious messianic passage. Rejoice! Rejoice!

"Look, your king will come to you.
    He is righteous and victorious" (Zechariah 9:9).

We are ready to hear that. The prophets have been honoring kings and princes; Judah is on the rise; the governor is praised as the "signet ring" of God (Haggai 2:23). But wait. What is this strange, upside-down phenomenon? He comes "humble and riding on an ass" (Zechariah 9:9). The messianic oracle shows a peaceful king, not like the greedy, haughty rulers of an earlier Judah. Now the peace of God will come as a servant king, a shepherd king so humble that he rides the lowliest beast of burden, his feet nearly touching the ground. How the ways of the world are reversed by the ways of God. God, mighty warrior, will conquer with a Messiah servant, humble and just. Jesus, in a calculated effort to interpret his servant kingship, lived out this prophecy by riding into Jerusalem on a donkey. What a picture of messianic humility in Zechariah! What an act of messianic humility in Jesus Christ!

Blood of My Covenant

God or the representative of God will be pierced (Zechariah 12:10). Blood will flow. The house of David will mourn. All Israel will mourn. Blood, for the Jews, meant life, the sanctity of life, life linked to the Lifegiver. Zechariah refers to "the blood of your covenant" (9:11). It will "release your prisoners." A sacrifice of blood on the altar as a guilt offering was life crying out to the Lifegiver for peace of soul. Such was the experience on the Day of Atonement (Leviticus 16). The great suffering servant passage in Isaiah 53 declares that innocent suffering is an expiation for the sins of others (Isaiah 53:5, 12).

Early Christians saw the messianic king riding on a donkey when Jesus entered Jerusalem. They also understood "the blood of your covenant" declared by Zechariah, which would "release . . . prisoners" as the blood of the crucified Christ poured out to free men and women from their sins. For Christians, Jesus on the cross fulfills the innocent blood sacrifice of Isaiah 53:5, ushers in the new covenant of Jeremiah 31:31, and pours forth a river of grace to the depths of the earth's need (Ezekiel 47:1-12).

Will the messianic shepherd be well received? No! The flock will not follow. The shepherd breaks his staffs into pieces (Zechariah 11:7-14). The wage they offer him—thirty shekels of silver—was the price of a slave (11:12-13).

What is Zechariah saying? Sin is deeper than imagined; it has a near stranglehold on the world. Why has the kingdom of righteousness not come? Because of incomprehensible human resistance. So these latter chapters of Zechariah respond to earlier dreams that had dissipated. Do not abandon hope. God is mightier even than sin. God will finally triumph.

Imagine you were a prophet in Judah during the period after the Exile. Haggai and Zechariah had encouraged the rebuilding of the Temple (Haggai 1:7-8; Zechariah 8:9). Ezra and Nehemiah had come along later to rebuild and strengthen the city walls and to bring reform through return to the law of Moses (Nehemiah 2:17; 8–9). The returned exiles, living under the relaxed policies of Persia, were trying to keep the Law. They had learned much from their experience in exile. Their social injustices, their mixing their religious practices with pagan gods, and their flirting with foreign alliances had cost them dearly. Through suffering, they learned that God's righteousness judges the nations, even Israel and Judah. They also learned God travels with the chariots; God was present even in Babylon. Pressed into their experience was the certain truth that God's constant compassion would never abandon them. Just as God had rescued Israel from Egypt, so God, with a second Exodus, had made a highway in the desert (Isaiah 40:3) to bring them home.

Not only had they rebuilt the Temple; they were trying to keep it ceremonially clean. No pagan gods were present. Only carefully

NOTES

prescribed rituals of sacrifice were offered. Tithes and offerings were brought to the Temple (Malachi 3:10).

Now they knew they were called to be a distinct people, a holy nation. But that presented real problems, for they lived among all sorts of peoples from all over the Near East. The Judeans who had survived the slaughter and stayed in Judah had intermarried and developed local customs. The Jews who returned from Babylon had to share the soil and participate in the economic and social life with people whose allegiance to Israel's God was at least compromised by other commitments. How could they live a holy life in a polluted world without getting contaminated?

Ezra's answer was to focus on being a separated people. They must follow the laws of Exodus, Leviticus, Numbers, and Deuteronomy. False idols are a laugh. Had not Amos and Jeremiah, Obadiah, even Nahum, shown that God would judge all the nations?

If the nations are recipients of God's judgment, are they not also recipients of God's salvation? Isaiah had said the rulers of all the nations would see the works of the Lord (49:7). God was performing a new Exodus; everyone would watch.

Israel was not only called to be God's saved people; Israel was called to be the agent of God's salvation for the whole world. Israel was called to be a witness, a light or blessing to the world.

It would have been easy for God simply to rescue Israel from captivity. But God had a much bigger plan in mind.

> "I have a greater task for you, my servant.
>   Not only will you restore to greatness
>   the people of Israel who have survived,
> but I will also make you a light to the nations—
>   so that all the world may be saved" (49:6, GNT).

God, with infinite compassion, *hesed* (steadfast love), will not be satisfied until the whole world is saved (45:22-23).

The Prophet Jonah

Now pretend you, as a prophet, know that the religious establishment thinks of the God of Israel in exclusive terms. What would you do to proclaim your message of salvation to the whole world? You might tell a story so poignant it could penetrate closed ears. Or you could begin writing about a prophet named Jonah.

There had been a prophet named Jonah who lived in the Northern Kingdom during the time of King Jeroboam II. The writer's selecting this earlier prophet as the central figure in the Book of Jonah was a great choice because of the meaning of his name. Jonah means "dove."

Jonah is still under the umbrella of God's power. Jonah, in the bottom of the sea, was as far from Mount Zion, the Temple, and Jerusalem as he could get; yet God was with him.

How long was Jonah in the belly of the deep? Long enough to sing one of the great liturgical psalms of Israel (Jonah 2:2-9). The last line is the clincher: "Deliverance belongs to the LORD!" (2:9).

Nineveh, the Gentile World

We are beginning to realize that Nineveh represents the whole Gentile world, all the foreign nations.

God wanted Israel, the messenger of truth and righteousness, to be a "light to the nations" (Isaiah 49:6). Why? In "Nineveh, that great city, . . . there are more than one hundred and twenty thousand persons who can't tell their right hand from their left" (Jonah 4:11). In the Gentile world, often so foreign and sometimes so alien and hostile, God was at work. The messenger of covenant love and law, Israel, must go to the Ninevehs of this world. Why? "That my salvation may reach to the end of the earth" (Isaiah 49:6).

If you had been a prophet in Israel around 400 BC, you could have put this amazing story into the minds of the people, keeping Israel's mission and God's ultimate purpose alive.

MARKS OF OBEDIENT COMMUNITY

A faith community is a hope-filled community. The Spirit has come down so that our young see visions and our old dream dreams. Both daughters and sons give testimony of God's love and power. We praise God, not because life is easy but because God is faithful.

The Israelites were called to be an "obedient community." They often failed. The prophets came as God's messengers to bring them back to obedience. Overall, what is the main message you have heard from the prophets?

What message do you hear that encourages you to be in an obedient community?

IF YOU WANT TO KNOW MORE

Trace the tithe through the Scriptures. Notice its spiritual and material elements.

Mark of Obedient Community
An obedient community lives in hope, Spirit-filled, with vision because God is faithful. They offer the compassionate, forgiving love of God to all persons and leave the judging to God.

Timeline of Old Testament Biblical Events

Dates are very approximate.

2000 BC	Patriarchs: Abraham, Isaac, Jacob
1700 BC	Joseph rules Egypt, Hebrew people go to Egypt
1300 BC	Egyptian captivity (Moses Born)
1260 BC	Exodus, desert wanderings
1220 BC	Conquest of Promised Land, period of the judges
1020 BC	United Kingdom: King Saul, King David, King Solomon (Temple built)
922 BC	United Kingdom divides into Israel and Judah
722 BC	Northern Kingdom of Israel conquered by Assyria (Assyrian exile)
	People exiled throughout Assyrian Empire
587/ 586 BC	Southern Kingdom of Judah (Jerusalem) conquered by Babylon, Temple destroyed, people exiled)
539 BC	Persia conquers Babylon: Persian Empire begins
538 BC	Persian king Cyrus allows exiles to return (first migration)
521 BC	Persian king Darius allows second migration of exiles to return
515 BC	Temple rebuild completed in Jerusalem
333 BC	Greek period, Alexander the Great
198 BC	Seleucid period
167 BC	Hasmonean period
63 BC	Roman Empire

Rulers and Prophets of Israel and Judah

Dates vary according to source. All dates are BC and are approximate.

United Kingdom

Year	King	Good or Evil	Prophets
1020–1000	Saul	Good	Samuel
1000–961	David	Good	Nathan
961–922	Solomon	Good/Evil	

Divided Kingdom

Israel (Northern Kingdom)				Judah (Southern Kingdom)			
Year	**King**	**Good or Evil**	**Prophets**	**Year**	**King**	**Good or Evil**	**Prophets**
922–901	Jeroboam 1	Evil	Ahijah	922–915	Rehoboam	Evil	
901	Nadab	Evil		915–913	Abijam	Evil	
900–877	Baasha	Evil		913–873	Asa	Good	
877	Elah	Evil					
876	Zimiri Tibni (?)	Evil					
876–869	Omri	Evil		873–849	Jehoshaphat	Good	
869–850	Ahab	Evil	Elijah (870–850)				
850–849	Ahaziah	Evil					
849–842	Jehoram (Joram)	Evil	Elisha(850–800)	849–842	Jehoram	Evil	
842–815	Jehu	Evil		842	Ahaziah	Evil	
815–801	Jehoahaz	Evil		842–837	Athaliah	Evil	
801–786	Jehoash (Joash)	Evil		837–800	Jehoash (Joash)	Good	
				800–783	Amaziah	Good	
786–746	Jeroboam II	Evil	Amos (760 *Jonah* –750)	783–742	Uzziah	Good	The First Isaiah (742–700) (Isaiah of Jerusalem)
746	Zechariah	Evil	Hosea (755–732)				Micah (742–687)
745	Shallum (Jehoahaz II)	Evil					
745–738	Menahem	Evil		742–735	Jotham	Good	
738	Pekahiah	Evil					
737–732	Pekah	Evil					
732–722/21	Hoshea	Evil					
722/21	Fall of Samaria to Assyria			735–715	Ahaz (Jehoahaz)	Evil	
				715–687	Hezekiah	Good	
				687–642	Manasseh	Evil	
				642–640	Amon	Evil	
				640–609	Josiah	Good	Zephaniah (628–622)
				609	Jehoahaz II (Shallum)	Evil	Jeremiah (626–580)
				609–598	Jehoiakim	Evil	Nahum (before 612)
				598	Jehoiachin	Evil	Habakkuk (605)
				597–587	Zedekiah	Evil	
				587/86	Fall of Jerusalem to Babylon		Obadiah (after 587)

Prophets of the Exile (Babylonian captivity 587/86–538)

Jeremiah (626–580)
Ezekiel (597–570)
The Second Isaiah (Isaiah of the Exile) (550–539)
Daniel (605–535)

Prophets After the Exile (Persian Empire 539–330)

Haggai (520–515)
Zechariah (520–515)
Joel (Persian Empire between 539–330
Malachi (500–450)
The Third Isaiah (Isaiah after the Exile) (538–445)

Rulers of Neighboring Powers

Dates vary according to source. All dates are BC and are approximate.

EGYPT	
Shishak	945–924
So (?)	About 730
Tirbakah	690–664
Neco	610–595
Hophrah	589–570

DAMASCUS (ARAM, SYRIA)	
Ben-Hadad I	990–860
Ben-Hadad II	860–843
Hazael	846–796
Ben-Hadad III	796–770
Rezin	740–732
Fall of Damascus	732

ASSYRIA	
Ashurnasirpal II	883–859
Shalmaneser III	858–824
Shamshi-adad IV	823–811
Adad-nirari III	810–783
Shalmaneser IV	782–773
Ashur-dan III	772–755
Ashuri-nirari V	754–745
Tiglath-pileser III	744–727
Shalmaneser V	727–722
Sargon II	721–705
Sennacherib	704–681
Esar-haddon	680–669
Ashurbanipal	668–627
Sinsharishkin	626–612
Fall of Nineveh	612
Ashuruballit	612–609

BABYLON	
Nabopolassar	625–605
Nebuchadnezzar II	605–562
Evil-merodach	562–560
Nergal-sharezer	560–556
Labashi-marduk	556
Nabonidus	556–539
Belshazzar (co-regent)	556–539
Fall of Babylon	539

PERSIA	
Cyrus II	539–530
Cambyses II	529–522
Darius I	522–486
Xerxes I	486–465
Darius II	423–405
Artaxerxes II	404–359
Alexander the Great dominates Persian Empire	331